AMERICAN HAIR METAL

STEVEN BLUSH

PHOTO CONTRIBUTIONS
WILLIAM HAMES
EDDIE MALLUK
FRANK WHITE

FERAL HOUSE

American Hair Metal © 2006 Steven Blush & Feral House
All Rights Reserved

ISBN: 987-1-932595-18-5, 1-932595-18-X

Feral House
PO Box 90039
Los Angeles, CA 90039

www.feralhouse.com

Design: Bill Smith
Image Editing: Jodi Wille
Creative Consultant: George Petros

10 9 8 7 6 5 4 3 2

Printed in China

CONTENTS

6 WELCOME TO THE JUNGLE

8 YOUTH GONE WILD

10 ROOTS OF HAIR METAL

14 BOYS IN HEAT

20 LIVE IT UP

26 BLOW MY FUSE

32 LAY YOUR HANDS ON ME

40 NAUGHTY, NAUGHTY

46 COCKED AND LOADED

52 WHY DO YOU THINK THEY CALL IT DOPE?

54 BURNING LIKE A FLAME

62 THE RIGHT TO ROCK

68 HOME SWEET HOME

74 TURN ON THE ACTION

86 O.F.R. (OUT FUCKIN' RAGEOUS)

92 IS THIS LOVE THAT I'M FEELIN'?

96 READ MY LIPS

100 LETTERS

104 HEADED FOR A HEARTBREAK

112 NOTHIN' FOR NOTHIN'

114 THE HAIR BANDS

164 MORE ESSENTIAL HAIR CUTS

166 SOURCES

172 CREDITS

Previous page: Poison, Right: Michael Monroe

WELCOME TO THE JUNGLE

There was a time, not so long ago, when big-haired bands ruled the world, and flashy "power ballads" dominated the airwaves. Well-coiffed acts like Poison, Cinderella, and White Lion pushed the limits of male sexuality with spandex, hairspray and stiletto heels—in a cool way that even straight Rock dudes could get into. This book pays tribute to this extinct civilization, a once-proud culture felled by changing times.

Western music forms traditionally emphasize technical proficiency, emotion or message. Hair Metal was about gettin' laid and kickin' ass. If rock 'n' roll means sex, the Hair bands rang as the ultimate manifestation.

Hair Metal was the pinnacle of narcissism, hedonism, egotism and sexy abandon. Few precedents informed this scene: the fops and dandies of Victorian England had the look but not the energy; Liberace had the chops but the wrong genes; the '70s Glam bands had the attitude but were too infected by the gravity of the Blues.

For those of you willing to let your hair down (or fluff it up!), welcome to the ultimate celebration of Sleaze.

Please note this book includes no recent interviews. That decision was made after phone conversations with a few of the scene's key characters. Overall, those conversations lacked any cool insight. Perhaps the characters' past art embarrassed them (a pathetic dilemma), or they were afraid to reminisce about past debauchery (worried about what the wife and kids might think…). Back in the day, these guys were outta control rockers. But that was ages ago. The quotes and lyrics herein, all vintage, illustrate where they were coming from at the time.

When the modern media reflects upon the hair bands, it is always with a smirk, if not downright derision. This scribe has a true appreciation of the art form. I love this stuff. With the help of *American Hair Metal*, you may, too.

In Rock,
Steven Blush
New York City
July, 2006

King Kobra

YOUTH GONE WILD

The mid-'80s saw the rise of rock's most outrageous era.

Pop music's pomp and circumstance melted into a glittery, trashy stew of hot licks, hot guys and mind-blowing fashion. Big hair and striking makeup adorned a pantheon of faux-feminine straight white alpha males rockin' out with sonic assaults of anthemic, melodic Metal. The music fell somewhere between Bubblegum and Hard Rock. Critics called it "Glam Metal" or "Sleaze Rock"—today's experts refer to it (often in a disparaging manner) as "Hair Metal."

Hair Metal should not be confused with similar Rock stereotypes—like studs-and-leather headbangers or operatic Queen-style bombastists or denim-clad Jersey rockers—though those guys all had varying levels of big hair and loud stagewear, too. The Hair bands wrapped all such impulses together, and took it to another level. This audacious new school—led by bands like Poison, Cinderella, and Warrant—achieved multi-platinum success, and dominated MTV's glory days.

All discussions of previous pop/rock forms—be it Elvis, the Beatles, Punk, Rap, Grunge etc.—posit brash young rebels against a staid musical establishment, followed by the evolution of something new in their wake. Such revolution was not the case with Hair Metal.

Here was a form that was all about NOT doing something new. Its entire *raison d'être* was embracing clichés, particularly "Sex & Drugs & Rock & Roll." The music pushed classic Rock motifs to their limits, and yet presented the resulting sound as a suburban soundtrack. High-livin' and hedonism defined success, just as was the case with all previous rock stardom—but the Hair Metal guys took it to new extremes.

Tuff

"I'VE ALWAYS BEEN A BIG BELIEVER IN THE STAR SYSTEM—THE IDEA OF THE STAR BEING SOMETHING THAT PEOPLE EITHER LOOK UP TO OR LIVE THROUGH VICARIOUSLY."

—Paul Stanley, KISS (1988)

Above: KISS, Right: New York Dolls

THE ROOTS OF HAIR METAL

I'M THE KING OF THE NIGHTTIME WORLD
COME LIVE YOUR SECRET DREAM

—Kiss, "King of the Nighttime World"

Anything remotely heavy and melodic on the radio was fair game as an influence. Every Hair Metal band had varying degrees of Led Zeppelin, Aerosmith, AC/DC, KISS and Van Halen in them, and every frontman owed more than a little to the sexy swagger of Robert Plant and David Lee Roth. The stylistic precursor of a Hair band would probably be the late-'70s outfit Angel (with well-coiffed Punky Meadows and Greg Giuffria), labelmates and touring-mates of KISS, and the first to credit hair stylists in their LP liner notes. The first rock band to adopt the lipstick-transvestite look was the '70s Glam band, The New York Dolls. Late in the game, Poison and other Hair bands attributed their look to the Dolls, though it probably came from more commercial realms.

"THE EARLY '80s? COME ON! YOU HAD SOME DISPOSABLE INCOME AND YOU DIDN'T NEED TO WEAR A CONDOM— THAT RIGHT THERE GETS YOU THROUGH A HOLIDAY WEEKEND IN STYLE. I WAS AN ABSOLUTE REFLECTION OF THAT."

—David Lee Roth (1994)

"ROCK SHOULD BE SOMETHING THAT FUCKIN' RIPS."

—Sammy Hagar (1994)

Left: David Lee Roth of Van Halen, Above: Punky Meadows and Frank DiMino of Angel

BOYS IN HEAT

"WE LIKE TO PARTY AND TO HAVE SEX—THAT'S PRETTY MUCH ALL WE DO."

—Erik Turner, Warrant (1988)

WITH A ROCKET IN MY POCKET
I JUST HAVE ONE THING TO SAY

—Vinnie Vincent Invasion, "Do You Wanna Make Love"

Hair Metal's heroes were not hippies or hipsters. They certainly were not nerds—in fact, they were the opposite. The focal point of the scene was alpha males—assertive, athletic, attractive guys who got the girls. They had animal magnetism, not just because they looked great, but also because they actually seemed like colorfully plumed birds. Female fans loved the pseudo-androgyny masking raging testosterone, but straight male fans had a different agenda: they dug the music, but they also lived vicariously through their stars—especially the idea of their heroes getting "all these chicks."

"IT'S A PERFECT SITUATION——EVERYBODY'S GETTING THEIR ROCKS OFF."

—David Coverdale, Whitesnake (1989)

"IT'S TRUE, SEX AND DRUGS AND ROCK AND ROLL CAN KILL YOU—ONLY IF YOU NEVER GET ANY!"

—Sebastian Bach, Skid Row (1991)

Left: Marq Torien of BulletBoys
Right: Tommy Thayer and Jaime St. James of Black N' Blue

WE'RE THE BADDEST BOYZ AROUND
JUST WAIT-N-C WHEN WE PLAY IN YOUR TOWN

—Nitro, "Bring It Down"

"WE'RE A VERY EMOTIONAL BAND, SEXUAL BAND, MANLY BAND... IT'S JUST THE WAY WE ARE."

—Ray Gillen, Badlands (1990)

Left: Bobby Rock of Nitro, Right: Whitesnake

THIS IS THE SEXIEST MUSIC MY GUYS HAVE EVER BEEN INVOLVED IN, AND THEY ARE THE SEXIEST FUCKING MUSICIANS. WHEN THEY PLAY, IT'S SEX."

—David Coverdale, Whitesnake (1989)

17

"OUR MUSIC'S RAW, NASTY, SLEAZY. IT DRIPS OF SEX."

—Vince Neil (1987)

"EVERYTHING WE DO IS BIG AND MONSTROUS AND AGGRESSIVE. I MEAN, SEX IS LIKE AN ALL-NIGHT SESSION, NOT JUST A QUICKIE IN THE BATHROOM…"

—Nikki Sixx, Mötley Crüe (1990)

Left to right: Vince Neil and Nikki Sixx of Mötley Crüe, Eric Carrol of Roxx Gang, Joey DeMaio of Manowar.

YOU KNOW WHAT TIME IT IS?
IT'S TIME TO GET WILD!

—Y&T, "Contagious"

These bands—by-products of the happy-go-lucky '80s—provided an energetic party vibe. They were pure entertainers—no tortured artist trip or subversive political intent, no stewing over Reaganomics, El Salvador death squads, nuclear holocaust, or any of society's other ills. They just cranked out cheeky double-entendre with the occasional paean of encouragement to someone who was feeling down. Warrant singing "Cherry Pie" or BulletBoys begging to "Smooth Up In Ya" encapsulate the one-track mindset.

Above: Warrant

LIVE IT UP

"THAT'S THE REASON YOU GET
INTO A ROCK BAND, RIGHT?
TO GET LAID AND TO GET
FREE BOOZE."

—Vince Neil, Mötley Crüe (1988)

Above: Jon Bon Jovi and fans, Right: Warrant

"WE JUST WANNA GO OUT AND KICK 100% OF EVERYBODY'S ASS IN THE AUDIENCE. THAT'S WHAT IT'S ALL ABOUT."

—Sebastian Bach, Skid Row (1989)

"I GOT INTO ROCK & ROLL TO GET GIRLS. I KEPT SEEING ALL THESE UGLY GUYS IN ROCK & ROLL WITH ALL THESE WOMEN, AND FIGURED I WAS NO UGLIER."

—Erik Turner, Warrant (1989)

"WE'RE GLADIATORS—PIRATE,
HIPPIE GLADIATORS.
EVERYONE WANTS TO PARTY
WITH US AND GET WILD."

—Stephen Pearcy, Ratt (1987)

Above: Ratt, Right: Bret Michaels of Poison

IF WANTING THE GOOD LIFE IS SUCH A CRIME LORD, THEN PUT ME AWAY!

—Poison, "Nothing But A Good Time"

BLOW MY FUSE

"WE DO GET MALE GROUPIES—LOTS OF THEM. BUT THEY'RE NOT AS BLATANT. GUYS DON'T GRAB. AND A LOT OF THEM GET SO NERVOUS WHEN THEY ASK FOR AUTOGRAPHS—THEY SHAKE. IT'S KIND OF FUNNY BUT I DON'T WANT TO LAUGH BECAUSE IT'LL EMBARRASS THEM."

—Roxy Petrucci, Vixen (1989)

ROLL OUT THE CARPET, AND KNEEL ONTO THE GROUND
SHUT OFF THE PARTY 'COS WE'RE COMING 'ROUND

—Vixen, "Hell Raiser"

The role of women was cut-and-dried. Sexual service and objectification came with the territory. The scene was driven by hot-blooded men livin' like rock stars who expected to get treated accordingly; women flocked, and the members obliged. Sex was the valued commodity, more important than the music in some cases. Objectification also meant a lack of respect for the scene's handful of kick-ass female musicians. Ex-Runaways guitarist Lita Ford attained success only after she sexualized her act; the same occurred, on smaller levels, for Vixen, Femme Fatale, and Poison Dollies.

26

28

Above: Poison Dollies, Right: Precious Metal

30

Above: Princess Pang, Right: Femme Fatale

LAY YOUR HANDS ON ME

"I REMEMBER IT BEING
SO NATURAL FOR THERE
TO BE 50 GIRLS IN ANY
CITY NAKED BACKSTAGE.
NO ONE WOULD THINK
TWICE ABOUT ANY OF IT."
—Tommy Lee, Mötley Crüe (1997)

SHE'S NOT THE KIND OF GIRL YOU BRING HOME TO MOM SHE'S MY HEAVY METAL LOVE

—Helix, "Heavy Metal Love"

Hair Metal came on at the onset of AIDS, yet continued to promote '60s/'70s Rock decadence. Sordid activities took place in hotel rooms, on the tour bus and backstage. The bands put considerable effort into getting chicks—Ratt's tour bus had a condom vending machine, and Poison traveled with their "groupie computer." A typical tour contract asked for a dozen condoms backstage, usually set in a bowl on a table next to the picked-over deli tray, celery sticks and potato chips. Porn Star girlfriends were only one of the trappings of hair metal stardom. Groupies, bedazzling in spandex and stilettos and overwrought hairspray, enthusiastically gave what they could—though in retrospect, the road crew, with their gifts of band access and backstage passes, received the lion's share of the gratification.

Warrant and friend

**"WE'VE ALREADY
SCREWED EVERY
GIRL IN L.A...I
DID A LOT OF
SOCIAL WORK!"**
—"Wild" Mick Brown, Dokken (1987)

"I PREFER BLONDES
SPREAD OUT ON
A WHOLE PIE. BUT
I EAT BRUNETTES
BY THE SLICE."
—Paul Stanley, KISS (1986)

**"MOUTH, HAIR,
LEGS, THE REAR.
MAINLY THE
MOUTH, THOUGH."**
—Vince Neil, Mötley Crüe (1987)

Left: Mick Mars of Mötley Crüe with friend, Right: porn star Lois Ayres (right) and friend, Far Right: Kix with groupie

"WE COME INTO TOWNS, MAKE
FRIENDS, GET WELCOMED
WITH OPEN ARMS, AND
HOPEFULLY, OPEN LEGS."
—Sebastian Bach, Skid Row (1990)

"WE USE, BUT WE GET USED, TOO. WE DO! WOMEN USE US AS MUCH AS WE USE THEM. IT'S A TOTALLY HONEST EXCHANGE."
—Rikki Rocket, Poison (1991)

"THERE'S AS MANY MALE GROUPIES AS THERE ARE FEMALE GROUPIES, IT'S JUST THAT THE FEMALE GROUPIES ARE MAGNIFIED BECAUSE THEY HAVE TITS AND AN ASS. THE MALE ROCK & ROLL GROUPIES ARE HIPPER THAN THE FEMALE ONES, BUT THE FEMALE ONES WILL DO THINGS TO YOU THAT YOU JUST WOULDN'T WANT THE MALES TO DO."
—Chip Znuff, Enuff Z'nuff (1993)

"I LIKE BOOBS, SO I TAKE BRAS. I DON'T TAKE UNDERWEAR."
—Taime Downe, Faster Pussycat (1988)

37

Left: Gene Simmons of KISS, Above: Steve Lynch of Autograph and friend

"IF BY A GROUPIE YOU MEAN A GIRL THAT FUCKS ANY GUY JUST BECAUSE HE'S IN A BAND——IF THAT'S WHAT IT IS——THEN I LOVE IT! OTHERWISE, I'D NEVER GET ANY!!"

—Rikki Rocket, Poison (1989)

"BATHROOM SEX IS SOMETHING I'VE BEEN GETTING A LOT OF LATELY, ESPECIALLY IN RESTAURANTS AND CLUBS AND STUFF... HALF THE REASON I GOT INTO THIS BUSINESS IS TO GET LAID AS MANY TIMES A DAY AS I CAN."

—Davy Vain, Vain (1989)

38

Metal photographer Frank White and friends

39

PANTIES 'ROUND YOUR KNEES
WITH YOUR ASS IN DEBRIS

—Guns N' Roses, "Anything Goes"

Sexual activity on the scene was rampantly hetero, but tame by modern standards—the most extreme incidents reported reeked of puerile misogyny. Sex with minors was routine but rarely prosecuted, though the L.A. band Nitro was put out of commission after guitarist Michael Angelo (Batio) was convicted of raping a 13-year-old in his tour bus (*Union-News,* Springfield, MA, 1/26/93). Alternative lifestyle questions came to light years later with the AIDS deaths of Ratt guitarist Robbin Crosby and Badlands singer Ray Gillen, and the sex change operation of King Kobra frontman Mark Free (who now performs under the name Marcie Free). The Rock persona demanded a Rock 'n' Roll road-warrior machismo that some could only live up to for so long.

40

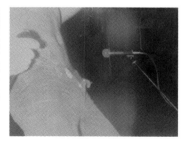

Above: fans, Below: fan photo

NAUGHTY, NAUGHTY

"IT'S A LITTLE TAMER THAN I THOUGHT IT WOULD BE. I THOUGHT IT'D BE A LOT WILDER. GIRLS COME AND BAKE YOU COOKIES AND BROWNIES...I DON'T UNDERSTAND IT, WE'RE BAD AS HELL."

—Kelly Nickels, L.A. Guns (1988)

"I CAN HONESTLY SAY THAT NOBODY PARTIED HARDER
THAN MÖTLEY CRÜE. ANY STORY YOU'VE HEARD OF THEM
IS PROBABLY NOT CRAZY ENOUGH... AFTER A WHILE, IT
WASN'T ABOUT SEX ANYMORE FOR THE GUYS BECAUSE
THEY HAD SO MUCH OF IT. IT BECAME ABOUT WHO COULD
DO THE WILDEST STUFF. I REMEMBER THEY'D GET GIRLS
TO DO STUFF LIKE HAVE THE PHONE RECEIVER UP INSIDE
THEM AS THEY WOULD CALL THEIR MOTHERS."

—Corky Gunn, Sweet Pain

Left: Mötley Crüe crew and groupies, Right: Steven Sweet of Warrant

"BEFORE I GO ONSTAGE, I DRINK THREE BEERS, DO A SHOT OF JACK DANIELS, TEN JUMPING JACKS, GO GET PUMPED UP AND LISTEN TO LOUD MUSIC. AFTER THE SHOW, I DRINK THREE MORE BUDWEISERS, GET MY CLOTHES ON, FIND SOME GIRLS IN THE CROWD, AND PROCEED TO HAVE A LOVELY EVENING ON THE TOUR BUS!"

—Jerry Dixon, Warrant (1989)

"SOME CHICK TOOK HER CLOTHES OFF IN FRONT OF OUR TOUR BUS ON THE ROAD. I MEAN EVERYTHING! THIS CHICK WAS NUDE IN THE CAR IN FRONT OF US WITH THE HATCHBACK DOWN. IT'S THE MOST AMAZING THING WE'VE EVER SEEN!"

—Kip Winger, Winger (1989)

43

"OUR TOUR BUS IS LIKE OUR PIRATE SHIP—IT'S WHERE WE RAPE AND PILLAGE. I WANT TO MAKE SURE OUR FEMALE FANS KNOW HOW TO BEHAVE. RATT IS ONE BIG ROCK & ROLL PARTY AND WHEN ANYONE HOPS ABOARD OUR TOUR BUS, THEY BETTER KNOW WHAT TO EXPECT."

—Stephen Pearcy, Ratt (1987)

"THE BIBLE LISTS THE SEVEN SINS THAT GOD HATES MOST— AND SEX ISN'T ONE OF THE SEVEN!"

—Robert Sweet, Stryper (1989)

"I THINK THE MOST DISAPPOINTING THING ABOUT BEING ON THE ROAD HAS BEEN SEEING HUNDREDS OF 14-, 15-, 16-YEAR-OLD GIRLS SPREADING THEIR LEGS EVERY NIGHT FOR ANYBODY WHO WANTS THEM. IT'S VERY DEGRADING AND UPSETTING. I MEAN, I DON'T GET OFF ON ABUSING TEENAGE GIRLS, I FEEL SORRY FOR 'EM. A LOT OF TIMES AT HOTEL PARTIES, I'LL SEE THESE 14-YEAR-OLD VIRGINS, AND I'LL TELL 'EM TO GO HOME. I'LL CALL 'EM A CAB, SO THEY DON'T END UP SLEEPING WITH ONE OF THE ROADIES OR SOMETHING."

—Ron Keel, Keel (1985)

"THIS GIRL COMES BACKSTAGE AND GRABS ME. SHE'S LIKE, 'OH MY GOD! I WANT TO FUCK YOU! I WANT TO FUCK THE WHOLE BAND!' ME BEING FUCKED UP, I SET A BOTTLE OF CHAMPAGNE ON THE GROUND AND SAID, 'TAKE OFF ALL YOUR ALL CLOTHES.' YOU THINK YOU'VE GOT SOME GOD-LIKE POWER OVER THIS PERSON. I TOLD HER TO SQUAT ON THE BOTTLE AND DON'T MOVE BECAUSE, 'I'LL BE RIGHT BACK BUT IF YOU MOVE THE DEAL'S OFF AND YOU AIN'T GETTING ANY OF THE BAND.' I CAME BACK AN HOUR LATER AND SHE'S STILL THERE WAITING. YOU THINK, 'DOESN'T THIS PERSON HAVE ANY SORT OF COUTH?' THOSE DAYS, PEOPLE DIDN'T REALLY GIVE A FUCK."

—Tommy Lee, Mötley Crüe (1997)

"I'LL GET STRAIGHTENED
OUT SOON. THE EXCESS
HAS GOTTEN TO BE
TOO MUCH... I'VE JUST
GOT TO LEARN TO
TAILOR IT DOWN."

—Bret Michaels, Poison (1989)

Left: Bret Michaels of Poison, Right: Kasey Smith of Danger Danger with friends

COCKED AND LOADED

THE ONLY TIME I TURN IT DOWN
IS WHEN I'M SLEEPIN' IT OFF

—Autograph, "Turn Up The Radio"

Alcohol and cocaine were the drugs of choice, and could always be found in abundance on the scene. Used in combination and in excess, they are key ingredients for an all-night Rock & Roll party. Similar to how the hippies discovered insight through LSD and the punks said "fuck the world" with amphetamines, a Hair band's illicit activities reflected its world view (cocaine is the drug of the self-absorbed and self-deluded). It's also the drug of the nouveau riche, and insane amounts of money were wasted on blow. Jack Daniels, vodka and beer washed away the coke drip —and washed away all inhibitions, both for the musicians onstage, and for females "hanging out."

47

"I AM ALWAYS READY TO PARTY. NO MATTER HOW TIRED MY BODY IS, I'M ALWAYS THE LAST ONE UP. I'M AFRAID I'M GONNA MISS SOMETHING!"

—"Wild" Mick Brown, Dokken (1987)

Left to right: Dokken, Mark Slaughter, Tracii Guns of L.A. Guns

"I DON'T HURT ANYBODY AND I DON'T FEEL I'M HURTING MYSELF. IF EVERYBODY'S CLEANING UP THEIR ACT, IT DOESN'T MEAN WE'RE GONNA JUMP ON THAT BANDWAGON."

—Kelly Nickels, L.A. Guns (1990)

"JACK DANIELS, COGNAC, RED AND WHITE WINE, CHAMPAGNE AND BACARDI—OUR BARS ARE COMPLETELY STOCKED!"

—Mark Slaughter, Slaughter (1990)

49

"I DON'T KNOW ONE BAND IN L.A.
THAT WASN'T DOING COKE."

—Don Dokken, Dokken (1991)

"PUKING IS THE SECOND BEST RELEASE TO ORGASM. I DIG IT. WHEN I PUKE, IT'S TOTALLY RIGHTEOUS. IT'S SO GREAT, IT'S LIKE A TOTAL RELEASE OF HEAVINESS. IT'S LIKE AN ORGASM COMING OUT OF YOUR MOUTH. IT'S SEXUAL."

—Sebastian Bach, Skid Row (1991)

Left: Members of Ratt and Britny Fox backstage with friends,
Right: Sebastian Bach of Skid Row

"I DON'T GET DRUNK, I GET SMASHED. I HATE THINGS DILUTED—I MEAN, YOU DON'T MIX JACK DANIELS WITH COKE. THAT'S A SIN."

—Nikki Sixx,
Mötley Crüe (1987)

"'FUCKING GREAT! GIVE ME THAT DRUG! YEAH, I'LL TAKE THAT ONE, TOO! FUCK IT, I DON'T CARE, I'LL EAT IT!' THAT'S THE VIBE."

—Vince Neil,
Mötley Crüe (1988)

WHY DO YOU THINK THEY CALL IT DOPE?

NAME-DROPPING NO-NAMES GLAMORIZE COCAINE

—Mötley Crüe, "Wild Side"

Mötley Crüe personified '80s excess. They walked the walk. But depending on which interview they conducted, they either frankly admitted, or vehemently denied, a decadent lifestyle. The denials often came at the behest of sound legal and business advice, but rang hollow. Below is a year-by-year breakdown of these big-haired ne'er-do-wells in action:

'85 "THE FANS UNDER-STAND THAT THE DRUGS, THE SEX, THE DRINKING AND THE EXCESSIVE LIFESTYLE ARE REFLECTED IN MÖTLEY CRÜE'S MUSIC."

—Nikki Sixx

'86 "WE JUST WANNA GET LAID AND GET WASTED."

—Nikki Sixx

'87 "I DON'T DO DRUGS! I THINK DRUGS ARE BAD."

—Nikki Sixx

'88 "WE REALLY THRIVE ON THE WORD 'SLEAZY.' EVERYBODY HAS GROUPIES, GETS DRUNK, DOES DRUGS. EVERYBODY HAS WILD SEX. WE'RE JUST VERY HONEST. WE ADMIT IT."

—Nikki Sixx

"I DON'T DO DRUGS. I DON'T DO DRUGS! I WISH PEOPLE WOULD GET THAT THROUGH THEIR HEADS."

—Nikki Sixx

'89 "I WAS TOTALLY ADDICTED TO HEROIN, AND WENT THROUGH REHAB..."

—Nikki Sixx

"REHAB WAS HELL! KICKING DRUGS SEEMED IMPOSSIBLE TO DO..."

—Nikki Sixx

'90 "KICKING DRUGS HAS BEEN AS EXCITING AS GETTING STRUNG OUT ON THEM USED TO BE."

—Nikki Sixx

"YEAH, THE FIRST REHAB DIDN'T WORK..."

—Nikki Sixx

"EVERY DAY I WANT A DRINK. I FEEL LIKE A TIME BOMB, LIKE I'M GONNA SNAP AT ANY MOMENT. I SHOULD SAY 'FUCK THIS!' BUT I'M TRYING TO KEEP IT TOGETHER..."

—Tommy Lee

53

"IF I WANNA PLASTER
LIPSTICK ON MY FACE
AND USE A WHOLE CAN
OF HAIRSPRAY, THAT'S
WHAT I'M GONNA DO!"
—Davy Vain, Vain (1989)

BURNING LIKE A FLAME

**I'M WEARIN' LEATHER HEAD-TO-TOE
GOT ME A MISSION,
AND MY MISSION IS TO ROCK & ROLL**
—Vain, "Aces"

The participants dressed with a particular pseudo-androgyny that excited the girls—and the straight guys thought it looked cool, too. In spandex and heels, with lipstick and teased hair, in flashy colors like hot pink, cherry red and lime green, the bands made an art form of posing and preening. However, Hair Metal should not be confused with queer culture—it had little in common with Oscar Wilde, fops, dandies, or *bon vivants*. The participants were not intellectuals or sophisticates and they were definitely not transvestites; they were simply blue-collar uber-heteros who dressed sorta like chicks because that's what got 'em laid. Amped on beer and blow, they'd be geared n' primed to kick your ass for calling 'em "fags" or "trannies."

Davy Vain of Vain

55

56

"WE'RE NOT GAY OR ANYTHING—WE JUST THINK WE LOOK BETTER WITH MAKE-UP."

—C.C. DeVille, Poison (1988)

"WE'RE NOT ASHAMED OF A LITTLE HAIRSPRAY AND MAKEUP. WE'VE ALWAYS SAID IT TAKES A REAL MAN TO WEAR MAKEUP."

—Bret Michaels, Poison (1988)

"WE ARE DEFINITELY IMAGE-
CONSCIOUS. BUT IT'S
HONEST—WE ALWAYS
DRESS THE WAY WE FEEL."
—Eric Brittingham, Cinderella (1988)

Left: Poison, Above: Robert and Michael Sweet of Stryper

58

IT'S NOT REALITY
IT'S JUST A FANTASY

—Aldo Nova, "Fantasy"

"ROCK 'N' ROLL IS ALL
ABOUT FANTASY, MAN.
IT'S SOMETHING NOT
EVERYBODY CAN DO."

—Kevin Steele, Roxx Gang (1989)

"I HATE IT WHEN
OTHER BANDS SAY
THEY DON'T GIVE A
SHIT ABOUT IMAGE.
WHAT A PILE OF
POOP THAT IS!"

—Bret Michaels, Poison (1988)

Left: Jim Gillette of Nitro, Right: Roxx Gang

"WE'D ALWAYS USED AQUA NET HAIRSPRAY. THAT WAS THE HAIRSPRAY FOR THE HAIR BANDS BECAUSE IT WORKED LIKE GLUE. YOU WOULD TURN YOUR HEAD UPSIDE DOWN SO YOUR HAIR HUNG DOWN, AND SPRAY LIKE CRAZY, THEN MAT IT DOWN AND SHAPE IT A BIT. YOU'D END UP LOOKING LIKE A CHICK, BUT THE GIRLS REALLY DUG IT."

—Corky Gunn, Sweet Pain

"WE THOUGHT WE HAD TO BE TOUGH BECAUSE WE DRESSED IN WOMEN'S CLOTH-ING. WE WOULD GET DRUNK AND HIGH AND WANT TO FIGHT WITH ANYONE."

—Corky Gunn, Sweet Pain

Left: Taime Downe of Faster Pussycat, Right: Mark Kendall of Great White

"I CAME HERE FROM LONDON WITH 200 BUCKS AND A HAIRDRYER."

—Phil Lewis, L.A. Guns (1988)

61

THE RIGHT TO ROCK

YOU GOT IT—
THE RIGHT TO ROCK!

—Keel, "The Right To Rock"

These bands claimed no ancillary spark in terms of breaking with convention—there was no political intent, independent spirit or DIY aesthetic. These guys got into it for the glory, and it was not uncommon if they had the stagewear and gear in place before their music even began to develop. Big-time managers and major labels execs pulled the strings—sometimes even creating the bands from scratch—with all aspects of creativity framed by the marketplace, and success judged by proximity to the tried-and-true Bubblegum-fused formula.

"WHAT WE'RE DOING HERE IS STRICTLY BLUE-COLLAR ART. WE'RE NOT CLASSY PEOPLE—BUT I BET WE HAVE MORE FUN THAN THEY DO."

—Rikki Rocket, Poison (1987)

62

Right: Rikki Rocket of Poison

"NOBODY IN THE
BAND GRADUATED
HIGH SCHOOL.
WHAT DO I NEED A
DIPLOMA FOR?"
—**Vince Neil, Mötley Crüe (1987)**

65

Vince Neil, Mötley Crüe

"I'M NOT OUT TO CONFUSE ANYBODY
WITH CONCEPTS. NOT TRYING TO SAY
ANYTHING EXCEPT, 'LET'S ROCK!'"

—Ron Keel, Keel (1987)

**"I'M UP ONSTAGE AND PEOPLE
ARE TOTALLY INTO IT FOR
A REASON—BECAUSE I'M
FUCKIN' GREAT AT WHAT I DO."**

—George Lynch, Dokken (1988)

Above: Keel, Left: Dokken

HOME SWEET HOME

"WE ALWAYS GIVE
JESUS CHRIST
A GOLD OR
PLATINUM ALBUM
WHEN THE BAND
EARNS ONE. HE'S
CERTAINLY A PART
OF THIS BAND."

—Michael Sweet, Stryper

ARE YOU TIRED OF WORKING 9 TO 5?
ARE YOU FED UP WITH YOUR BORING LIFE?

—White Lion, "Don't Give Up"

Hair Metal was a conservative art form. With its melodic appeal and frat-boy lyrics, parallels can be drawn to Easy Listening à la Ray Conniff and Percy Faith. Like Easy Listening, Hair Metal was the soundtrack of vanilla suburbs. The bands, marketed as from "New York" and "Los Angeles," were in fact born of mall-culture environs: New Jersey, Long Island and The Valley. A majority of the "L.A." bands were in fact transplants who relocated to "Hollywood" to find stardom.

Left: Juan Croucier of Ratt, Above: Stryper

"THIS IS THE WEIRDEST FUCKING BAND! NO ONE DOES COCAINE OR ANYTHING LIKE THAT. NO ONE FOOLS AROUND. THERE'S NO CHICKS ON THE TOUR BUS, THERE ISN'T EVEN A PORNO MOVIE ON THE BUS! IT'S SO FUCKING MELLOW, IT'S UNBELIEVABLE..."

—Vivian Campbell, Whitesnake (1988)

"WE CAN PARTY WITH
THE BEST, WE CAN ROCK
WITH THE BEST. BUT
WE'RE HIGH ON LIFE."
—Mike Tramp, White Lion (1988)

**"ALL THE GUYS HAVE THEIR
PARENTS' BLESSING.
NO, WE ARE NOT REBEL
MUSICIANS."**
—Dave "Snake" Sabo, Skid Row (1989)

Left: Whitesnake, Right: Mike Tramp of White Lion

71

"I JUST BROKE UP WITH MY GIRLFRIEND OF THREE YEARS, SO NOW I CAN FINALLY WRITE SONGS ABOUT SOME OF THE WILD SEXUAL THINGS THAT HAVE GONE ON IN MY LIFE. I COULDN'T DO THAT BEFORE."

—Jani Lane, Warrant (1990)

"I GUESS MY ONLY REAL VICE IS GIRLS... NO, NO IT'S MY CAR. I HAVE A 280Z."

—Jon Bon Jovi, Bon Jovi (1986)

Left: Jani Lane of Warrant, Right: Cinderella

"I'M RELIGIOUS. I STUDY THE BIBLE EVERY NIGHT."
—Fred Coury, Cinderella (1987)

The players' ethnic profile read as White, particularly WASP, with a few high-profile Italian-American guitar virtuosos—Steve Vai (David Lee Roth/Whitesnake), Warren DiMartini (Ratt), Richie Sambora (Bon Jovi), Vito Bratta (White Lion)—and Cuban-born bassists Juan Croucier (Ratt) and Rudy Sarzo (Ozzy, Quiet Riot, Whitesnake). Top Jewish entertainers like Kiss and David Lee Roth inspired Hair Metal's Borscht Belt vibe, but Semitic play in the movement was minor (Bon Jovi keyboardist David Bryan [Rashbaum], Danger Danger singer Ted Poley) but offset by all the Jewish lawyers, managers, and record company employees working behind the scenes. African-American input was non-existent—the scene was a respite from soul, and the one or two Black metalheads in each town were the ultimate outcasts. In the end, Hair Metal was a White art form—like oil and water, Aqua Net and afros never mixed.

Left: Danger Danger, Above: Bon Jovi

Left: Minoru Niihara of Loudness, Right: EZO

The few foreign acts who found success on the scene were wannabe American-style bands who took inspiration from U.S. Rock and fed into the zeitgeist of the day: big-haired kids cruisin' Sunset Strip, partyin' in the parking lots of The Roxy, The Rainbow, and Gazzarri's. Sexy Scandinavians excelled at the genre: Hanoi Rocks (Finland), an inspiration for Guns N' Roses; striking White Lion frontman Mike Tramp (Denmark); and Swedish acts Europe, Shotgun Messiah, Electric Boys, TNT (with American singer Tony Harnell), and guitar hero Yngwie Malmsteen, who came to prominence on The Strip in proto-Hair bands like Alcatrazz and Steeler. The Japanese made waves with Loudness and the Gene Simmons-produced EZO. The U.K., where Glam ruled in the '70s, was noticeably absent, weighing in with Tigertailz (the "Welsh Poison") and the Stones/Faces-style Dogs D'Amour and London Quireboys.

"OBVIOUSLY THERE HAVE BEEN MORE GIRLS THAN BOYS IN MANY PLACES WE PLAY. I KNOW THE GUYS KNOW NOT TO IGNORE US BECAUSE OF THAT!"

—Ian Haugland, Europe (1988)

Left: Michael Monroe of Hanoi Rocks, Right: Europe

80

Analysis aside, what ultimately sold the Hair bands to the masses was their songs. Here were loud, aggressive, melodic Metal acts who sold out clubs and moved 100,000 units on their own kick-ass credentials, but million-seller stardom only came with the delivery of radio-ready tearjerkers. The "power ballad," a prescribed blend of metal guitar crescendo and syrupy love cry, inspired by the mega-success of Zep's "Stairway To Heaven" and "Dream On" by Aerosmith, became the sonic path to victory. "Home Sweet Home" by Mötley Crüe and Poison's "Every Rose Has Its Thorn" are examples of high-energy party bands tempered for Top 40 success with platinum hit power ballads.

81

Mötley Crüe

82

A **major-label** feeding frenzy broke out circa 1987 in the wake of the runaway success of Guns N' Roses and Poison. Every label ran a sizable stable of pseudo-androgynous rockers. For every winner (Warrant, Slaughter) came a dozen flops (Rock City Angels, Hericane Alice, Vinnie Vincent Invasion, Beau Nasty). These acts boasted in interviews of their "multi-album, multi-million-dollar deals" that were in fact heavily backloaded and guaranteed only one or two albums, making it simple for labels to axe their turkeys. To paraphrase, the philosophy was to sign ten bands, and if one of the ten hit big, the profit would more than cover any loss on the other nine. There was so much money being made, it was crazy.

The explosion of bands arose from overlapping and interlocking social, management, and talent pools: for example, L.A. Guns came out of Guns N' Roses; Britny Fox from Cinderella, and the Ratt-Dokken-Quiet Riot pollination reads as such: Ratt drummer Bobby Blotzer played with Don Dokken, replaced by future Quiet Riot drummer Frankie Banali; bassist Juan Croucier left Dokken to join Blotzer in Ratt; Ratt guitarist Warren Di Martini (for whom Warrant is "named after") replaced George Lynch in Dokken when Lynch tried out for Ozzy; and future Ozzy guitarist Jake E. Lee played in early Ratt with singer Stephen Pearcy on rhythm guitar. The fact that everyone partied and played together made the musicians even more integrated and interchangeable.

Left: Beau Nasty, Right: Cinderella

For around 75,000 '80s dollars, an inner circle of studio producers could deliver a slick, big-sounding album that opened with a raucous Rock anthem and included one or two power ballads as well as at least one track that displayed the guitarist's virtuosity. Knobtwisters like Beau Hill (Ratt, Winger, Warrant), Michael Wagener (Dokken, Skid Row, White Lion), and Tom Werman (Mötley Crüe, Whitesnake, Kix) came in huge demand. If any problems arose, the labels employed an array of outside writers (like Desmond Child), stand-in players (the Ponti brothers), and remixers (Thompson and Barbiero) to save the day.

In response arose a cottage industry of independent marketing specialists (McGathy, Concrete) who could be hired, for top dollar, to get the bands into heavy rotation on Rock radio (KNAC, Z-Rock radio network) and push their big-budget, big-haired videos onto MTV (*Dial MTV, Headbanger's Ball*). Hit after hit further institutionalized a strict blueprint for success.

Publishers that churned out glossy *Teen Beat*-style publications launched new titles dedicated to the hotties of Hair Metal—*Hit Parader, Rip, Circus, Metal Edge, Rock Scene, Metallix,* et cetera—widely distributed in the shopping malls, supermarkets and convenience stores of the Heartland. The magazines, filled with major record label ads, fed into the perception of these guys as rich, high-livin' heartthrobs.

The bands can be divided into distinct image types (though most successful artists went through most/all of these phases): "Glam" bands, like a safer version of the New York Dolls, in women's clothing and overdone makeup (Poison, Tuff, Pretty Boy Floyd); "Frilly" bands, with fluffy duds inspired by Elizabethan England or the court of Louis XIV (Cinderella, Britny Fox); "Heartthrob" bands, dressed like cute guys from the mall, in parachute pants and Capezios (Winger, Bon Jovi); and the "Biker" bands, dressed bad-ass, but with lotsa hairspray (L.A. Guns, Faster Pussycat). As time went on, many of the Hair bands tried to toughen their image—often with disastrous results.

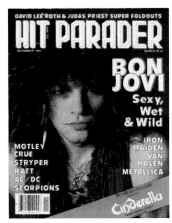

"THE GOAL WE HAD WAS TO CONQUER THE WORLD, AND WE DID IT. NOW WE'RE LOOKING TO BE POPULAR ON OTHER PLANETS. INTERGALACTIC STARDOM..."

—Stephen Pearcy, Ratt (1987)

MY TONGUE'S TALKIN' RIDDLES
BUT I JUST CAN'T SEEM TO FIND A CLUE

—Mötley Crüe, "City Boy Blues"

Overnight fame and fortune, rampant intoxication and unbridled sexual attention made for mind-boggling cases of self-delusion and self-importance. Even modest levels of success led to enormously swollen heads, and bodacious claims of invincibility.

86

Ratt

O.F.R. (OUT FUCKIN' RAGEOUS)

YOU GOT TO KNOW
THAT I'M WILD YOUNG AND CRAZY
—Hericane Alice, "Wild Young And Crazy"

"I'M NOT WORRIED ABOUT OUR AUDIENCE DISAPPEARING, BECAUSE WE CAN ALWAYS COUNT ON OUR FANS."

—Kevin DuBrow, Quiet Riot (1985)

'OUR SONGS ARE GONNA LAST FOREVER..."

—Vito Bratta, White Lion (1989)

"IF I DIED RIGHT NOW, I'D BE A HERO IN ROCK AND ROLL. I'LL ALWAYS BE REMEMBERED AS THE FIRST TO OPEN THIS CATEGORY FOR WOMEN AS HARD ROCKERS. AND THAT WILL MAKE ME LIVE FOREVER."

—Lita Ford (1989)

89

Left: Hericane Alice, Right: Rudy Sarzo and Kevin Dubrow of Quiet Riot

"SOMEDAY WE'LL BE KNOWN AS ONE OF
THE BIGGEST BANDS IN THE WORLD."

—Tony Harnell, TNT (1986)

**"OUR BAND'S GOAL IS TO BE WHERE
CINDERELLA IS NOW. NOTHING IS
GONNA STOP US!"**

—"Dizzy" Dean Davidson, Britny Fox (1987)

Above: Tony Harnell of TNT, Right: Michael Sweet of Stryper

"I SEE OUR GROUP REACHING THE TOP AND STAYING THERE FOR A LONG TIME..."

—Michael Sweet, Stryper (1986)

"BEAU NASTY REPRESENTS EVERYTHING I'LL EVER NEED. WE WILL BE AROUND FOR A LONG TIME TO COME."

—Mark Anthony Fretz, Beau Nasty (1990)

KIP WINGER

"I CAN SEE US OVER A LONG PERIOD OF TIME BEING LIKE QUEEN, JETHRO TULL OR YES."

—Kip Winger, Winger (1988)

91

IS THIS LOVE THAT I'M FEELIN'?

I'M A KNOCK-DOWN, DRAG-OUT SON OF A BITCH JUST HELL-RAISING MOTHER WITH A BURNING ITCH

—McQueen Street, "When I'm In The Mood"

Beefs between bands or band members is certainly nothing new. For the Hair bands, unbridled egotism, juvenile behavior, raging hormones, drugged fantasy, and too much time in front of a mirror all contributed to high-profile pissing matches between artists. Most dirty laundry was publicly aired, splashed across the pages of glossy Metal mags and/or highlighted on "MTV News."

**WHITESNAKE
JOHN SYKES VS. DAVID COVERDALE:**

"WHEN YOU'RE WITH DAVID COVERDALE, HE MAKES YOU FEEL LIKE YOU'RE HIS BEST FRIEND. AND WHEN HE'S FINISHED WITH YOU, HE'LL NEVER TALK TO YOU AGAIN."

—John Sykes, ex-Whitesnake, Blue Murder (1989)

"IT MADE SENSE FOR ME TO WEED OUT THE DEADWOOD AND THE NEGATIVE INFLUENCES IN MY LIFE, PERSONAL AND PROFESSIONAL. NOW THERE ARE NO PASSENGERS RIDING ON THE H.M.S. WHITESNAKE."

—David Coverdale, Whitesnake (1989)

RATT VS. POISON:

"THERE'S NO POISON THAT CAN KILL RATT."

—Stephen Pearcy, Ratt (1987)

POISON VS. GUNS N' ROSES:

"WE REALLY HATE POISON—THEY TOTALLY EMPHASIZE EVERYTHING WE HATE IN A BAND!"

—Slash, Guns N' Roses (1987)

"GUNS N' ROSES USED TO WEAR MORE MAKEUP THAN POISON EVER WORE, AND LIKE A YEAR LATER THEY HAVE ON THEIR PANTS, 'GLAM SUCKS.'"

—Bret Michaels, Poison (1990)

Poison

MÖTLEY CRÜE VS. BON JOVI:

"HOW DO I FEEL ABOUT BON JOVI'S COMMERCIAL BREAKTHROUGH? GREAT! THEY'RE FRIENDS OF OURS."

—Nikki Sixx, Mötley Crüe (1987)

"BON JOVI IS EVERYTHING CORPORATE ABOUT ROCK & ROLL THAT WE DON'T RESPECT."

—Nikki Sixx, Mötley Crüe (1997)

94

Nikki Sixx of Mötley Crüe

DON DOKKEN VS. EVERYONE

"ROCK & ROLL IS SUPPOSED TO BE FUN, [PLAYING IN] DOKKEN WASN'T."

—Juan Croucier, Ratt (1986)

"I HAVE A REPUTATION FROM SOME PEOPLE THAT I'M COCKY, ARROGANT, AND HARD TO GET ALONG WITH..."

—Don Dokken, Dokken (1991)

"IT WAS KIND OF HARD TO GET USED TO, BUT I THINK WE'VE WORKED IT ALL OUT. I'VE ALREADY STRANGLED DON A FEW TIMES!

—"Wild" Mick Brown, Dokken (1986)

"THERE IS SOME FRICTION HERE. WHAT I TRY TO AVOID IS THE EGO TRIPS—WHEN YOU START BECOMING SUCCESSFUL, WHEN THE GUYS IN THE BAND START TO BELIEVE THEIR OWN HYPE AND THE ARTICLES..."

—George Lynch, Dokken (1987)

"GEORGE AND I HATE EACH OTHER. WE'RE NOT BEST OF FRIENDS. WE SEE THINGS DIFFERENTLY IN LIFE. BUT IT'S LIKE SIBLING RIVALRY."

—Don Dokken (1986)

"I THINK A LOT OF THE PROBLEM IS THAT I WAS ON DRUGS IN THE EARLY DAYS OF DOKKEN, AND I WAS JUST NUTS—NEUROTIC, DOING COCAINE. EVERYONE WAS. AND ANYONE WHO SAYS WE DIDN'T DO DRUGS IS A LIAR.

—Don Dokken (1991)

95

"JUST FOLLOW YOUR HEART AND FOLLOW YOUR INSTINCTS. AND IF SOMETHING TELLS YOU THAT YOU NEED A PROPHYLACTIC WITH THIS LOVELY YOUNG LADY, THEN USE IT!"

—Marq Torien, BulletBoys (1989)

"NEVER FUCK ON BALCONIES, ESPECIALLY IF YOU'RE DRUNK."

—Jani Lane, Warrant (1990)

96

READ MY LIPS

"WHAT HAVE I LEARNED? USE A RUBBER AND CHECK I.D."

—Bret Michaels, Poison (1987)

I REMEMBER WAY BACK WHEN I WAS JUST LIKE YOU YEAH I GAVE MYSELF TO LIVE BUT I DIDN'T HAVE A CLUE

—L.A. Guns, "Electric Gypsy"

The bands struck a peculiar image, at once rock sluts and role models. Virtually every decadent band partook in anti-drug media campaigns, like "Just Say No" or the D.A.R.E. program—the most egregious example being the "Moscow Peace Festival" with Mötley Crüe, Skid Row, Bon Jovi, Cinderella and Ozzy Osbourne, a debaucherous affair produced by manager Doc McGhee, as part of his public service on a marijuana distribution guilty plea. Nearly every interview conducted with these artists included a question that asked them to advise the kids—ironic, as these dudes were too fucked up to find the door, let alone to lead by example.

97

Left: Marq Torien of BulletBoys, Right: Bret Michaels of Poison

"OUR PHILOSOPHY? HAVE FUN, GET LAID, GET DRUNK..."

—Steven Sweet, Warrant (1988)

"OUR PHILOSOPHY IS THAT WE'RE DANGEROUS BUT WORTH THE RISK."
—Stephen Pearcy, Ratt (1989)

Left: Warrant, Above: Ratt

This is for Nikki Sixx,
I want you to know you are the best bass player and a great songwriter. You're also very, very sexy. Actually, you're the sexiest man in my life. I'd have all your children if you'd ask me. I went to your concert in New Haven where Tommy Lee fell. My dad was at the show too, and he said you were very professional and talented, which is great compliment from a guy who likes very prudish groups. I also admire you for kicking drugs. That's a great accomplishment!
Melissa F.
Woodbury, CT
(*Hit Parader,*
November 1990)

I had to write about the interview with Bret Michaels in your October issue. I think he is great, musically and personally. Besides being the sexiest man in the world, he's so down to earth and easy-going. He really cares about his fans, and it hasn't all gone to his head. To all those assholes who call Poison glam fags, please give it up and quit being jealous just because you're not making the bucks. Don't get me wrong, I'm a sincere headbanger—I like everything from Testament and Metallica to Mötley Crüe and GN'R— but really respect Bret for his integrity and compassion for what he's doing. Tell him I love him and keep it rockin'!
Sheri R.
Topeka, KS
(*Rip,* January 1991)

I RECENTLY WROTE YOU A LETTER ABOUT JON BON JOVI NOT BEING A HOMOSEXUAL. I WANTED TO THANK YOU FOR PRINTING IT. I HAD MY CHANCE TO PROVE TO EVERYBODY THAT THEY WERE WRONG.
Tina F.
Newport News, VA
(*Blast,* June 1989)

Fan art, left to right: Bret Michaels, Poison; Tom Keifer, Cinderella; Jon Bon Jovi; Nikki Sixx, Mötley Crüe

For all of Nikki Sixx's talk, he didn't say enough about the new album. One thing I really took notice of was Nikki's sexual references in most of the songs. No, I don't take offense, I just wish I was there to inspire him!

Lee Ann C.
Whitefish, Canada
(*Circus,* January 1990)

My name is Danny and I'm 13 years old. Yes, I would like to see more of Tawny Kitaen. There's nothing I want less of in your magazine. I feel good with hard rock. My favorite band is Whitesnake, my idols, Guns N' Roses. Thanks for printing this.

Danny B.
San Diego, CA
(*Metallix,* May 1988)

David Coverdale of Whitesnake should be arrested for obscene sexual gestures. And we want to be the arresting officers!

The Sex Police
Wichita, KS
(*Hit Parader,* January 1987)

I am deployed in the Persian Gulf onboard the U.S.S. Detroit. I'd like to say it's bands like Poison, Crüe and Skid Row that keep us rockin' during this ordeal. Thanks and keep up the good work.

Matthew K.
U.S.S. Detroit
(*Circus,* May 1991)

THIS IS IN RESPONSE TO WHAT VINCE NEIL, LEAD SINGER OF MÖTLEY CRÜE, SAID ON MTV, THAT "GROUPIES ARE REAL SLEAZY, AND ALL THEY WANNA DO IS FUCK YOUR BRAINS OUT." WELL, MAYBE THAT'S TRUE, BUT THERE ARE SOME OF YOUR FEMALE FANS THAT JUST WANT TO MEET YOU AND TELL YOU HOW THEY FEEL ABOUT YOUR MUSIC. REMEMBER, THOSE SO-CALLED "SLEAZY" GIRLS MADE YOU AND CRÜE WHO YOU ARE TODAY. ALL BANDS SHOULD RESPECT THEIR FANS. WITHOUT US, YOU'D BE NOTHING.

Mary M.
Tabb, VA
(*Circus,* June 1987)

HAIR FAN LETTERS

I am appalled by your article on Winger. This article contains quote after quote about Kip's interest and concern for his fans. What a crock! Kip is distant, rude, self-centered, and certainly not interested in "spending time with each fan, finding out what they do." I had the displeasure of meeting Kip at a backstage gathering before his last show on tour with Cinderella. When my friend asked him for his autograph, he took our papers and signed them with an "I don't need this shit" look on his face. Kip strutted around like he was the most important thing around. Kip was the guy I was most excited about meeting, and his behavior was a slap in the face. I learned that rock stars are just actors and nobody special when they're not on stage.

T.D.
Lewiston, ME
(*Circus*, June 1989)

WE WENT TO SEE MÖTLEY CRÜE IN EAST RUTHERFORD, NEW JERSEY. WE WERE SHOCKED WHEN THEY PLAYED INSTRUMENTS THAT SAID, "KILL BON JOVI." WE WOULD LIKE THEM TO KNOW THAT THEY CAN'T LIVE THIS DOWN! THEY CAN'T JUST WALK INTO A BAND'S HOME STATE AND MAKE FUN OF THEM. YOU ARE LOSING YOUR BEST FANS!

Two ex-Crüe Fans
Monmouth, NJ
(*Rip*, April 1990)

Richie Sambora and George Lynch are bitchin' guitarists but Aldo Nova is the best, better than Malmsteen and Van Halen. How about an article on my favorite band White Lion?

Cub
Ft. Lauderdale, FL
(*Metal Edge*, December 1987)

Whoever said that girls can't play is screwed. One of my favorite guitar players is Lita Ford, and her looks have nothing to do with it. I'm a guy and I say that women rockers kick ass. If it wasn't for the likes of Lita Ford, Girlschool, Precious Metal and Poison Dollies, there would be hardly any true metal.

David L.
Sweetwater, TX
(*Circus*, July 1988)

I was deeply disturbed by your interview with Stryper…I found it very offensive—grow up and show respect…Personally, I adore them and am very excited they are here…

Betsy H.
Canoga Park, CA
(*Powerline,* July 1989)

My friends and I think Sebastian Bach, Rachel Bolan, Nikki Sixx, Tommy Lee, Jerry Dixon, Eric Turner, Jani Lane, Vince Neil, Bret Michaels, Steven Adler, Duff McKagan, Axl Rose, and the drummer of Danger Danger are some of the hottest guys we would love to #*@%@ !!! Keep it up dudes!!

M.D., D.F, J.D.
North Jersey
(*Powerline,* May 1990)

YOU HAVE A BLACK AND WHITE PICTURE OF STEPHEN PEARCY IN THE OCTOBER ISSUE, WHERE HE'S DRESSED IN SKIN TIGHT LEATHER PANTS AND WHERE I CAN SEE THE OUTLINE OF STEPHEN PEARCY'S ----- THROUGH SKIN TIGHT LEATHER PANTS, WHICH LOOKS LIKE HE HAS A 9-INCH -----. I WISH STEPHEN PEARCY WAS MY ROOMMATE, SO I COULD PLAY WITH HIS ----- WHILE SQUEEZING HIS ----- THROUGH HIS SKIN TIGHT LEATHER PANTS. I'D LOVE TO TAKE HIM IN MY ARMS AND KISS HIM ON THE LIPS AND HUG HIM FROM BEHIND, SO THAT MY ----- IS AGAINST STEPHEN'S -----.

Gayly Yours,
Fred B.
Milwaukee, WI
(*Creem,* February 1986)

Fan art, left to right: Stryper; White Lion; Guns n' Roses; Stephen Pearcy, Ratt

103

HEADED FOR A HEARTBREAK

CINDERELLA

YOU DON'T KNOW WHAT YOU'VE GOT TILL IT'S GONE
DON'T KNOW WHAT IT IS I DID SO WRONG

—Cinderella, "Don't Know What You've Got (Till It's Gone)"

Every new generation develops its own new sound that replaces the previous generation's: The Beatles and the British Invasion killed off the Pat Boones, similar to how the Sex Pistols and the punkers dispensed with '70s stoner rock. So when Nirvana—whose 1991 explosion was the closest thing to Beatlemania in America thus far—came on the scene, along with all the Grunge and Alternative bands, MTV and the record labels saw the writing on the wall. There's never been another musical form like Hair Metal that sold so much, and evaporated so fast.

"ONE DAY, THIS IS ALL GONNA BE OVER. YOU'RE KIDDING YOURSELF IF YOU DON'T BELIEVE THAT."

—Don Dokken, Dokken (1986)

"GIRL AUDIENCES ARE FICKLE. THE YEAR WE CAME OUT, WE WERE COOL. THEN THEY DECIDED THEY LOVED SKID ROW. THEN WARRANT. NOW IT'S MARK SLAUGHTER. IT GIVES BANDS A WAY IN, BUT THOSE FANS DON'T STAY WITH YOU."

—Kip Winger, Winger (1991)

"THOSE WERE GOOD TIMES, BUT TIMES CHANGE. YOU GROW UP AND YOU MOVE ON..."

—Stephen Pearcy, Ratt (1989)

"THE KIDS DECIDE WHO LIVES AND WHO DIES, THUMBS UP OR THUMBS DOWN."

—Vince Neil, Mötley Crüe (1987)

Steven Pearcy of Ratt

I DON'T NEED TO BE THE KING OF THE WORLD
AS LONG AS I'M A HERO TO THIS LITTLE GIRL

—Warrant, "Heaven"

As the Hair bands built their careers on the backs of 14-year-old girls, their careers were a literal house of cards vulnerable to collapse from the winds of change (cultural and hormonal). In contrast, the Grunge and Alternative bands—products of the '80s Hardcore Punk scene—laid down deep roots by the early 1990s, so it was only a matter of time until one of these bands broke.

Top to bottom: fan with Bobby Rock, Vinnie Vincent and Dana Strum of Vinnie Vincent Invasion

"I THINK A LOT OF US FORGOT TO WRITE INTELLIGENT LYRICS. AND I POINT THE FINGER AT MYSELF, TOO. I THINK OUR WRITING BECAME VERY MUCH A FORMULA. AND WHEN THAT HAPPENS, THE MUSIC GETS STALE."

— Jani Lane, Warrant (1995)

"WE DIDN'T GET INTO THIS TO BE A POP BAND. WE WERE SUPPOSED TO BE A HEAVY ROCK BAND..."

—Sebastian Bach, Skid Row (1989)

"THERE ARE A HELLUVA LOT OF BANDS THAT ARE DOING THIS SACCHARINE, WIMPY, BALLADY STUFF——AND IT'S TOTALLY PLAYED OUT."

—Phil Lewis, L.A. Guns (1990)

"I HATE ALL THESE POWER BALLADS, I THINK THEY'RE REDUNDANT. BUT WHAT ARE YOU GONNA DO?"

—Tommy Lee, Mötley Crüe (1990)

"IT'S SO OBVIOUS—CAN'T KIDS REALIZE THAT THEY'RE SHOVING THIS SHIT DOWN THEIR THROATS?"

—Phil Lewis, L.A. Guns (1990)

"WHAT THE HELL DID YOU EXPECT? DID YOU THINK PEOPLE WOULD CONTINUE BUYING THIS PREPACKAGED PRODUCT FOREVER?

—Jani Lane, Warrant (1995)

107

The scene might've been able to weather the Alt Rock storm, had someone, anyone, stayed the course. But everyone seemed so insecure with the jokes and smirks that the whole thing dried up overnight. Was it all a mirage?

"MTV SUDDENLY BECAME LESS SUPPORTIVE, AND RADIO WAS ROUGH TOO BECAUSE THEY WERE PLAYING ALL KINDS OF MUSIC—GRUNGE AND ALTERNATIVE."

—Bret Michaels, Poison (1995)

"MTV TURNED ON US, RADIO TURNED ON US—THE INDUSTRY TURNED ON US LIKE RABID DOGS."

—Nikki Sixx, Mötley Crüe (1997)

"EVERYTHING'S FLIP-FLOPPED. ALL THE UNDERGROUND BANDS OF THE '80s THAT WERE ON LITTLE INDIE LABELS ARE NOW THE MILLION-SELLERS. AND ALL THE BANDS THAT WERE MILLION-SELLERS ARE NOW CULT BANDS."

—Vince Neil, Mötley Crüe (1995)

"I'LL NEVER FORGET WALKING INTO [COLUMBIA RECORDS PRESIDENT] DON IENNER'S OFFICE AND SEEING THIS HUGE POSTER OF ALICE IN CHAINS. I THOUGHT, 'HELLO SEATTLE...GOODBYE WARRANT.'"

—Jani Lane, Warrant (1995)

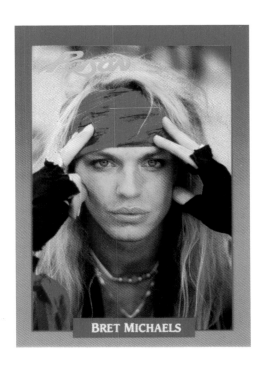

BRET MICHAELS

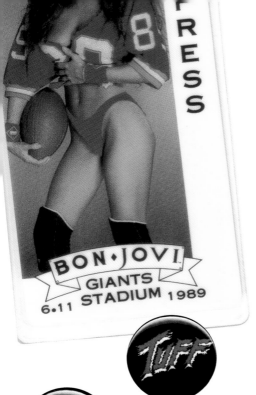

JON BON JOVI

WARRANT

While it is true that the music industry totally bailed on the Hair bands—even after those bands earned the fat cats millions of dollars—the bands themselves are also to blame, as they bailed on their sound and style, too. In doing so, they alienated their own scene and blue-collar fanbase.

Instead of staying true, hair metal bands tried to change with the times—and failed. Simply put, debaucherous big-haired boyz, by their own definition, could never be part of the Grunge generation. Warrant doing "Cherry Pie" dressed in flannel shirts and backwards baseball hats wasn't gonna work. Like the biblical tale of Samson and Delilah, these guys cut their hair, and lost their power.

The stigma of the Hair era was so severe that almost no one survived the transition—the only exception was the scene's biggest star Jon Bon Jovi, who was more than just a Rock singer and was destined for celebrity, whether he cut his hair and moved on or not.

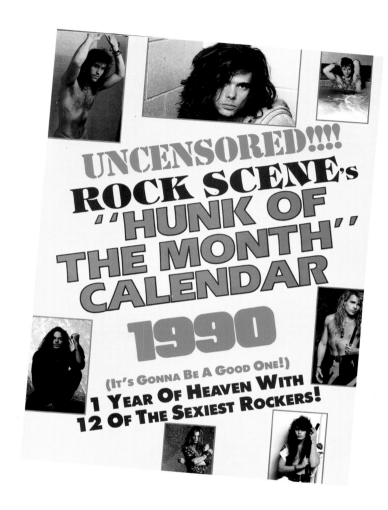

"THOSE HEAVY METAL DAYS OF FUN, SMOKING POT, CRUISING AROUND WITH FRIENDS, PICKING UP GIRLS—THOSE ARE ALL MEMORIES NOW..."

—Vinnie Vincent, Vinnie Vincent Invasion (1986)

"WHAT'S REALLY, REALLY IMPORTANT TO ME, WHEN ALL IS SAID AND DONE, IS THAT I HAVE MADE SOME MUSIC THAT MATTERS, SOMETHING I CAN BE PROUD OF. I DON'T KNOW IF WE HAVE DONE THAT UP TO THIS POINT."

—George Lynch, Dokken (1987)

"IT'S HARD TO REALIZE WE'RE TRYING TO BE PART OF SOMETHING WE AREN'T NECESSARILY PROUD OF."

—W. Axl Rose, Guns N' Roses (1988)

NOTHIN' FOR NOTHIN' (EPILOGUE)

"IF I'VE GOT ONE REGRET,
IT'S THAT I DIDN'T DO
THINGS DIFFERENTLY."
—Vinnie Vincent, Vinnie Vincent Invasion (1989)

THE HAIR BANDS

"MY BAND IS NOT WIMPY. I MEAN, COMPARED TO METALLICA IT'S WIMPY——BUT FUCK, WHO CARES ABOUT THEM?"

—Tommy Thayer, Black 'N Blue (1986)

GONNA POUND MY HEAT INTO YOUR MEAT

—Black 'N Blue, "The Strong Will Rock"

BLACK 'N BLUE

BIRTHPLACE: Portland, OR

BANDMEMBERS: Jaime St. James (vocals), Tommy Thayer (guitar), Jeff Warner (guitar), Patrick Young (bass), Pete Holmes (drums)

ESSENTIAL HAIR CUTS: "Hold On To 18," "The Strong Will Rock "

FASCINATING FACTS: Discovered by Don Dokken, who produced their first demo in 1983; Warner played in early bands with Metallica's Lars Ulrich, and the band debuted on the same *Metal Massacre* compilation that launched Metallica; hooked up with Gene Simmons in LA, where he produced their fourth album, 1988's *In Heat;* broke up in 1989 due to general lack of interest; Thayer went on to tour and record with Ozzy Osbourne; he can be seen playing in Kiss as the Ace Frehley "Space Ace" character.

116

> "JERSEY RULES!... ME AND BRUCE AND SOUTHSIDE JOHNNY, WE KNOW A LITTLE ABOUT THE STREETS."
>
> —**Jon Bon Jovi (1988)**

FROM NEW JERSEY TO TOKYO RAISE YOUR HANDS

—**Bon Jovi, "Raise Your Hands"**

BON JOVI

BIRTHPLACE: Sayerville, NJ

BANDMEMBERS: Jon Bon Jovi (vocals), Richie Sambora (guitar), Alec John Such (bass), Tico Torres (drums), David Bryan (keyboards)

ESSENTIAL HAIR CUTS: "Lay Your Hands On Me," "Bad Medicine," "In And Out Of Love," "Wanted Dead Or Alive"

FASCINATING FACTS: Jon, born John Francis Bongiovi, son of a florist and a hairdresser; as a teen, played the Jersey Shore bar circuit with Motown-style cover bands Atlantic City Expressway and The Rest (the latter's demos produced by Southside Johnny); swept floors, worked as a gofer at the Power Station for famous producer cousin Tony Bongiovi (Aerosmith, Ramones, Ozzy, etc); Sambora played in Mercy, signed to Led Zep's label Swan Song, but whose LP was shelved when John Bonham died; then he played for a year with Joe Cocker, where he teamed with Alec John Such; band wrote smash *Slippery When Wet* in seclusion in Richie's mom basement in South River, NJ; Sambora dated Cher, later married Heather Locklear; Jon dated Diane Lane, who he met through a blind date set up by Aldo Nova; later married high school sweetheart Dorothea Hurley in May 1989 at the Graceland Chapel in Vegas; March 15 is "Bon Jovi Day" in Sayreville.

"WE'RE TRYING TO CREATE SOMETHING NEW—SOMETHING LIKE AMADEUS MEETS MEGADETH."

—Michael Kelly Smith,
Britny Fox (1988)

BRITNY FOX

BIRTHPLACE: Philadelphia, PA
BANDMEMBERS: "Dizzy" Dean Davidson (vocals), Michael Kelly Smith (guitar), Billy Childs (bass), Johnny Dee (drums)
ESSENTIAL HAIR CUTS: "Girlschool," "Long Way To Love" "Standing In The Shadows"
FASCINATING FACTS: Michael Kelly Smith and drummer Tony "Stix" Destra, original members of Cinderella, were fired when that band signed to Polygram in 1985 (Destra died in a February 8, 1987 car accident); named for the Welsh coat of arms of one of "Dizzy" Dean Davidson's 18th century ancestors; band noted in metal circles for their 1987 demo *In America;* voted "Best New Band" of 1988 by the readers of *Metal Edge;* Davidson quit Britny mid-tour in 1990 to pursue his own band, Blackeyed Susan.

119

DON'T LET YOUR LOVIN' GO TO WASTE ALL IT TAKES IS JUST ONE DATE

—BulletBoys, "Smooth Up In Ya"

"TO ME, WE'RE MAKING MUSIC THAT STANDS THE TEST OF TIME."

—Marq Torien, BulletBoys (1991)

BULLETBOYS

BIRTHPLACE: Los Angeles, CA

BANDMEMBERS: Marq Torien (vocals), Mick Sweda (guitar), Lonnie Vincent (bass), Jimmy D'Anda (drums)

ESSENTIAL HAIR CUTS: "Smooth Up In Ya," "For The Love Of Money"

FASCINATING FACTS: Warner Bros. exec Roberta Peterson took her brother, Van Halen producer Ted Templeman, to see the band, he later produced the band's two VH-style albums, which included Metal covers of The O'Jays' "For The Love Of Money" and "Hang On St. Christopher" by Tom Waits; Sweda, Vencent and Torien played in Carmine Appice's King Kobra; Marq's dad trombonist in Stan Kenton's big band, his mom sang background vocals; Torien previously signed to the Motown Records R&B group Cagney and the Dirty Rats; BulletBoys were notorious for trashing hotel rooms.

CINDERELLA

BIRTHPLACE: Philadelphia, PA
BANDMEMBERS: Tom Keifer (vocals, guitar), Jeff LaBar (guitar), Eric Brittingham (bass), Fred Coury (drums)
ESSENTIAL HAIR CUTS: "Shake Me," "Nobody's Fool," "Gypsy Road," "Don't Know What You've Got ('Till Its Gone)"
FASCINATING FACTS: Philly cover band vets of acts like Saints In Hell and Priscilla Harriet Band; signed to Polygram after Jon Bon Jovi saw them play at the Empire Club in Philly in 1985; a "serious band" with no drinkin' and druggin' allowed; Beirut-born drummer Fred Coury never even heard Rock music until 1980; *Metallix* (#2, 1987) wrote: "the band was involved in a Cherry Coke concert giveaway and produced their own line of school supplies, including notebooks, folders and lunchboxes."

> **"I WAS IN THE BATHROOM OF THIS CLUB DOING MY HAIR, AND TOM CAME UP TO ME AND SAID, 'YOU WOULDN'T HAPPEN TO BE A BASS PLAYER?' THE NEXT DAY I WENT DOWN TO THAT SAME CLUB AND AUDITIONED, AND THEY SAID, 'YOU'RE COOL, YOU'RE IN THE BAND.'"**
>
> —Eric Brittingham, Cinderella (1988)

THAT DRESS YOU'RE WEARING
MAKES YOU LOOK SO CUTE
BUT GIRL, YOU'D LOOK BETTER
IN YOUR BIRTHDAY SUIT
—Danger Danger, "Naughty Naughty"

"WE'RE A CROSS BETWEEN
METALLICA AND THE
PARTRIDGE FAMILY."
—Bruno Ravel, Danger Danger (1989)

DANGER DANGER

BIRTHPLACE: Long Island, NY
BANDMEMBERS: Ted Poley (singer), Andy Timmons (guitar), Bruno Ravel (bass), Kasey Smith (keyboards), Steve West (drums)
ESSENTIAL HAIR CUTS: "Naughty Naughty," "Bang Bang"
FASCINATING FACTS: Ravel and West started the band in 1987, and hooked up with Imagine Records, the Epic-distributed label of Lenny Petze, who signed Boston, Cyndi Lauper and Aldo Nova; Ravel had previously backed up Michael Bolton and wrote "Temptation" for Y&T; Poley drummed in the Progressive Rock band Prophet, and sang at numerous Bar Mitzvahs, including his own; West was a top Long Island strip joint DJ.

"IF IT WASN'T
FOR THE FANS,
I'D STILL BE
WORKING
ON CARS."
—**Don Dokken, Dokken (1986)**

DOKKEN

BIRTHPLACE: Los Angeles, CA
BANDMEMBERS: Don Dokken (vocals), George Lynch (guitar), Jeff Pilson (bass), "Wild" Mick Brown (drums)
ESSENTIAL HAIR CUTS: "It's Not Love," "Burning Like A Flame," "Breaking The Chains," "Alone Again"
FASCINATING FACTS: Donald Maynard Dokken came to fame in Europe with his band Airborne, where he worked with Scorpions producer Dieter Dirks; Dokken debut LP came with a sticker that read "rhymes with rockin'." Don produced early demos/albums for Great White, Black 'N Blue, and XYZ; Dokken vs. Lynch, one of the great rock feuds, the band broke up many times, the first time in '88; Pilson left to front the short-lived War and Peace; Lynch and Brown went on to form Lynch Mob.

"YOU TAKE VAN HALEN, THE BEATLES AND CHEAP TRICK, PUT THEM ALL IN A BLENDER, AND YOU'VE GOT ENUFF Z'NUFF."

—Chip Z'nuff, Enuff Z'nuff (1990)

ENUFF Z'NUFF

BIRTHPLACE: Chicago, IL
BANDMEMBERS: Donnie Vie (vocals), Derek Frigo (guitar), Chip Z'nuff (bass), Vikki Foxx (drums)
ESSENTIAL HAIR CUTS: "New Thing," "Fly High Michelle"
FASCINATING FACTS: Donny and Chip met in 1984 in the Chicago suburbs, where Chip played minor league baseball; Chip briefly dated Madonna; Aerosmith loved their self-titled 1989 debut album, and wanted Enuff to be their opening act—until they saw what the chrome-glinted quartet actually looked like; Foxx quit to join Vince Neil's solo band; Frigo died of a drug overdose in May 2004; Chip still tours with a lineup of the band without Vie.

**SEX ON THE BRAIN
PUMPED IN MY VEINS
FLOWING FROM MY
HEAD TO MY FEET**

—Extreme, "Pornograffiti"

"WE DON'T POSE, AND
WE'RE NOT PRETTY...
WE'RE FOR REAL."

—Gary Cherone, Extreme (1990)

EXTREME

BIRTHPLACE: Boston, MA
BANDMEMBERS: Gary Cherone (vocals), Nuno Bettencourt (guitar), Pat Badger (bass), Paul Geary (drums)
ESSENTIAL HAIR CUTS: "Mutha," "Kid Ego," "More Than Words"
FASCINATING FACTS: Cherone and Geary had The Dream, that changed when ABC-TV bought the moniker for a show in development (with a young John Stamos) and became Extreme, as in "ex-Dream"; first Extreme gig was Sept. 14, 1985 at Bunratty's in Allston, MA; band signed to A&M in Nov. 1987; from blue-collar South Boston, the members represented the 'hood's ethnic Portuguese, Italian, and Irish communities; Azores-born Bettencourt was both a guitar god and a heartthrob (voted "Top 10 Sexiest Rockers" by *Playgirl*); A&M insured Nuno's fingers for $5M with Lloyd's Of London; monster ballad "More Than Words," off their second album *Pornograffiti*, became an early-'90s prom theme; Cherone played Jesus in a Boston production of *Jesus Christ Superstar,* and briefly sang for Van Halen.

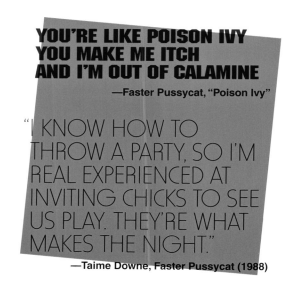

**YOU'RE LIKE POISON IVY
YOU MAKE ME ITCH
AND I'M OUT OF CALAMINE**

—Faster Pussycat, "Poison Ivy"

"I KNOW HOW TO THROW A PARTY, SO I'M REAL EXPERIENCED AT INVITING CHICKS TO SEE US PLAY. THEY'RE WHAT MAKES THE NIGHT."

—Taime Downe, Faster Pussycat (1988)

FASTER PUSSYCAT

BIRTHPLACE: Los Angeles, CA

BANDMEMBERS: Taime Downe (vocals), Brent Muscat (guitar), Greg Steele (guitar), Eric Stacy (bass), Mark Michals (drums)

ESSENTIAL HAIR CUTS: "Don't Change That Song," "Poison Ivy," "Bathroom Wall," "House Of Pain"

FASCINATING FACTS: Took their name from the Russ Meyer film, *Faster Pussycat! Kill! Kill!;* signed to Elektra in December 1986, allegedly within three weeks of band's formation; Taime once played in the Seattle band Bondage Boys, where he got his S&M nom-de-plume; Taime and "Headbanger's Ball" VJ Rikki Rachtman threw L.A.'s hottest Hair Metal parties at The Cathouse; Michals ousted from band after a Fed Ex package to him with heroin was intercepted by authorities; Faster played "last show" July 6, 1993; Taime went on to make Industrial Music with Pigface and Newlydeads (with Kyle Kyle of Bang Tango).

MY FINGERNAILS LEFT FIERY
TRAILS ACROSS YOUR BACK
TELL ME BABY, HOW'D YOU LIKE
THAT LITTLE PUSSY SCRATCH?

—Lita Ford, "Hungry"

LITA FORD

BIRTHPLACE: Los Angeles, CA
BANDMEMBERS: Lita Ford (vocals, guitar), Donnie
Nossov (bass), Myron Grombacher (drums), David
Ezrin (keyboards)
ESSENTIAL HAIR CUTS: "Kiss Me Deadly," "Close My
Eyes Forever"
FASCINATING FACTS: Born Carmelita Rossanna Ford in
London; played guitar with Joan Jett and Cherie Currie
in legendary all-girl band The Runaways; supported
herself as a beautician at the start of solo career;
fashion makeover and addition of Pop producer Mike
Chapman led to the smash "Kiss Me Deadly"; "Close
My Eyes Forever," hit duet with Ozzy, came together
as she worked with manager Sharon Osbourne; later
recorded an un-ironic cover of Alice Cooper's "Only
Women Bleed"; once married to Chris Holmes of
W.A.S.P., re-married to Jim Gillette of Nitro.

GONNA DRIVE MY LOVE INSIDE YOU GONNA NAIL YOUR ASS TO THE FLOOR

—Great White, "On Your Knees"

"IT'S A SLUMBER PARTY ON THE ROAD, EXCEPT WE DON'T WEAR NO PAJAMAS!"

—Jack Russell, Great White (1990)

GREAT WHITE

BIRTHPLACE: Los Angeles, CA

BANDMEMBERS: Jack Russell (vocals), Mark Kendall (guitar), Michael Lardie (guitar), Lorne Black (bass), Audie Desbrow (drums)

ESSENTIAL HAIR CUTS: "Rock Me," "Lady Red Light," "Face The Day"

FASCINATING FACTS: L.A. club vets, originally called Danté Fox; came to prominence working with Guns N' Roses manager Alan Niven; band famous for Grammy-nominated cover of Mott The Hoople's "Once Bitten, Twice Shy"; horrific incident Feb. 20, 2003 at The Station in Providence, RI, a pyrotechnics mishap sparked a fire that killed 100 people, including guitarist Ty Longley.

129

> "WE'RE SORT OF A SORE THUMB ON THE GLAM SCENE—IN THE MIDDLE OF IT, BUT AT THE SAME TIME, NOT INTO IT AT ALL..."
> —Slash, Guns N' Roses (1989)

> "I DON'T COPE WITH THINGS VERY EASILY."
> —W. Axl Rose, Guns N' Roses (1989)

GUNS N' ROSES

BIRTHPLACE: Hollywood, CA

BANDMEMBERS: W. Axl Rose (vocals), Slash (guitar), Izzy Stradlin (guitar), Duff McKagan (bass), Steven Adler (drums)

ESSENTIAL HAIR CUTS: "Welcome To The Jungle," "Paradise City," "Sweet Child O' Mine"

FASCINATING FACTS: Part of Hair scene in their early days, circa "Welcome To The Jungle"; W. Axl Rose, his real name William Bailey, once played in a band called Axl, and his natural father's last name was Rose; GN'R came out of Hollywood Rose, Axl's band with Tracii Guns—who left to form L.A. Guns; Slash (Saul Hudson) almost joined Poison instead; McKagan drummed in seminal Seattle Hardcore Punk band The Fartz; Duff relocated to L.A. and joined Road Crew, with Slash and Adler (a friend of Slash since skater days at Bancroft Junior High); Izzy Stradlin (Joseph Isabelle) was Axl's neighbor in their strict Pentecostal hometown of Lafayette, IN; after mega success of *Appetite For Destruction,* band went four years between studio albums, during which time they fired Adler (for drug reasons!) and went through a series of drummers: Fred Coury (Cinderella), Adam Maples (Sea Hags), Martin Chambers (Pretenders), Matt Sorum (The Cult).

LET'S GO SKIN TO SKIN IT'S TIME TO START GIVIN' IN

—Heaven's Edge, "Skin To Skin"

"WHAT WE GET TO DO EVERY NIGHT IS SO FUCKIN' COOL!"

—Mark Evans, Heaven's Edge (1990)

HEAVEN'S EDGE

BIRTHPLACE: Philadelphia, PA
BANDMEMBERS: Mark Evans (vocals), Reggie Wu (guitar, keyboards), Steven Parry (guitar), George "G.G." Guidotti (bass), David Rath (drums)
ESSENTIAL HAIR CUT: "Skin To Skin"
FASCINATING FACTS: One album of big-haired melodic Hard Rock for Columbia, and were dropped soon after the record's release; bassist George "G.G." Guidotti was shot by crazed fan after a show, and took 140 pellets to his right side, which he survived, and still had the lead in him as the band toured to support the record; broke up 1992 after a failed development deal with Capitol.

**WE ARE UNITED NATIONS
UNDER THE FLAG OF ROCK & ROLL**

—Keel, "United Nations"

"I WANT TO BE THE GUY TO PLAY
HEAVY METAL IN OUTER SPACE."

—Ron Keel, Keel (1987)

KEEL

BIRTHPLACE: Los Angeles, CA

BANDMEMBERS: Ron Keel (vocals, guitar), Marc Ferrari (guitar), Bryan Jay (guitar), Kenny Chaisson (bass), Dwain Miller (drums)

ESSENTIAL HAIR CUTS: "The Right To Rock," "Rock and Roll Outlaw"

FASCINATING FACTS: Ron Keel came to fame as the singer of Steeler, with a young Yngwie Malmsteen on guitar; Gene Simmons produced the two classic Keel albums (*The Right To Rock, The Final Frontier*); their career was directed by Danny Goldberg at Gold Mountain Records; "Rock and Roll Outlaw" was the theme to the cult film *Dudes;* after Keel, Ferrari went on to Cold Sweat, with one album for MCA; Ron went solo, first fronted an all-female band called Fair Game; then moved to Nashville and became Country artist Ronnie Lee Keel.

"I'VE BEEN IN THIS BUSINESS FOR QUITE AWHILE, SO TRUST ME WHEN I TELL YOU THAT KING KOBRA IS WHAT ROCK & ROLL IS ALL ABOUT."

—Carmine Appice, King Kobra (1988)

KING KOBRA

BIRTHPLACE: Los Angeles, CA
BANDMEMBERS: Mark Free (vocals), David Michael Philips (guitar), Mick Sweda (guitar), Johnny Rod (bass), Carmine Appice (drums)
ESSENTIAL HAIR CUTS: "Ready To Strike," "Mean Street Machine"
FASCINATING FACTS: With matching peroxide blonde manes, one of the wildest-looking bands of all time; the creation of legendary drummer Appice (Vanilla Fudge, Beck, Bogart and Appice, played on Rod Stewart's "Da Ya Think I'm Sexy"); Philips came from Keel; Sweda formed BulletBoys; singer Mark Free underwent sexual reassignment surgery, now singer Marcie Free.

135

KIX

BIRTHPLACE: Hagerstown, MD
BANDMEMBERS: Steve Whiteman (vocals), Ronnie Younkins (guitar), Brian Forsythe (guitar), Donnie Purnell (bass), Jimmy Chalfant (drums)
ESSENTIAL HAIR CUTS: "Cold Blood," "Girl Money," "Don't Close Your Eyes"
FASCINATING FACTS: Kings of the DC-Baltimore circuit that spawned Angel, Wrathchild (America), DC Star, and Child's Play; first called Shooez but changed their name because of the Midwest New Wave band The Shoes; Brad Diven quit Kix to form Wrathchild, later called Souls At Zero; band's chart success came with 1988's *Blow My Fuse,* and the power ballad "Don't Close Your Eyes"; Forsyth briefly replaced by Jimi K. Bones of NYC's Skin And Bones; Kix broke up in January 1996, after seven albums; one of the most underrated bands of the era.

"I DON'T DO SHIT. I DRINK A HELLUVA LOT OF BEER. I GUESS IT RUNS IN THE FAMILY."
—Steve Whiteman, Kix (1989)

L.A. GUNS

BIRTHPLACE: Los Angeles, CA

BANDMEMBERS: Phil Lewis (vocals), Tracii Guns (guitar), Mick Cripps (guitar), Kelly Nickels (bass), Steve Riley (drums)

ESSENTIAL HAIR CUTS: "No Mercy," "Electric Gypsy," "Rip and Tear," "The Ballad Of Jayne"

FASCINATING FACTS: Band formed after Tracii Guns split with Axl Rose, he was the "Guns" in Guns N' Roses; Lewis came out of the UK band Girl, which launched Phil Collen of Def Leppard; Nickels came from Faster Pussycat (after a bad motorcycle accident), he'd previously played in NYC with Angels In Vain and Sweet Pain; Cripps briefly played in Mercyful Fate; Steven Riley, who replaced Punk drummer Nicky Beat, had done three albums with WASP; the video to "The Ballad Of Jayne" (about Jayne Mansfield) shot at the former estate of Philippines dictator Ferdinand Marcos; Guns went on to the short-lived supergroup Contraband, with members of Ratt, Vixen and Shark Island.

> "BLACK HAIR IS A REQUIREMENT TO BE IN THIS BAND. AND YOU HAVE TO BE INSANE."
> —Tracii Guns, L.A. Guns (1988)

> "I REMEMBER THINKING, 'OH MY GOD, IF THIS BECOMES SUCCESSFUL, WHAT KIND OF MONSTER HAVE I CREATED?'"
> —Phil Lewis, L.A. Guns (1988)

MICHAEL MONROE

BIRTHPLACE: Helsinki, Finland/New York, NY
BANDMEMBERS: Michael Monroe (vocals), Phil Grande (guitar), Kenny Aaronson (bass), Thommy Price (drums)
ESSENTIAL HAIR CUTS: "Dead, Jail Or Rock 'N' Roll," "Man With No Eyes"
FASCINATING FACTS: Hanoi Rocks vocalist credited as godfather of the movement; moved to NYC, where he lived with Stiv Bators; king of NYC Hair Metal scenes at The Cat Club and The Limelight; in 1989 recorded *Not Fakin' It* (Mercury) with help of Little Steven and top Manhattan studio musicians; dropped by the label for being a prima donna because he complained about MTV ads that said "Michael Monroe's not fakin' it."

138

I'M NOT FAKIN' IT FOOLIN' MYSELF THAT I'M MAKIN' IT
—Michael Monroe, "Not Fakin' It"

"YOU BETTER LIKE SEX IF YOU GET INTO THIS BUSINESS, BECAUSE YOU'RE GONNA GET FUCKED A LOT!"
—Michael Monroe (1989)

"WE ARE MÖTLEY CRÜE TWENTY-FOUR HOURS A DAY, WHETHER I'M ON THE BEACH OR IN THE BACK OF SOMEBODY'S CAR WITH SOME SLUT."

—Nikki Sixx, Mötley Crüe (1986)

"I'M NOT GONNA BE 60 AND LOOK OVER AT VINCE AND SAY, 'I WISH WE SCREWED THAT CHICK...'"

—Nikki Sixx, Mötley Crüe (1988)

MÖTLEY CRÜE

BIRTHPLACE: Los Angeles, CA

BANDMEMBERS: Vince Neil (vocals), Mick Mars (guitar), Nikki Sixx (bass), Tommy Lee (drums)

ESSENTIAL HAIR CUTS: "Kickstart My Heart," "Dr. Feelgood," "Girls Girls Girls," "Shout At The Devil," "Live Wire," "Home Sweet Home"

FASCINATING FACTS: Vince Neil (Wharton), son of an L.A. County Sheriff's Office maintenance supervisor, his first band cover act Rock Candy; Vince killed Hanoi Rocks drummer Nicholas "Razzle" Dingley (and maimed two others) on Dec. 8, 1984 in Redondo Beach, when he totaled his 1972 Ford Pantera; served 30 days in June 1986 at Gardena City Prison for vehicular manslaughter and drunk driving, fined $2.7M, five years probation and 200 hours community service; Neil had a bit role in the Andrew Dice Clay film *Ford Fairlane* as Johnny Black, a rock star who gets murdered; *Rolling Stone* wrote that Vince would take steroid shots before going onstage; Aerosmith's "Dude (Looks Like A Lady)" is about Vince; Nikki's (Frank Carlton Serafino Ferrano) parents were traveling musicians who briefly played with Sinatra; he grew up in Seattle and at his grandfather's Idaho potato farm; got into Rock because his uncle was president of Capitol Records, and sent him Beatles records; Nikki dated Lita Ford early on; Vince has "USDA Choice" tattooed on his left buttock, Nikki has red puckered lips inked next to his crotch; Mars (Bob Deal) was a Country musician from Huntington, IN (birthplace of Dan Quayle); son of a Baptist minister and a Sunday school teacher; "T-Bone" Lee (Thomas Bass), Greek-born, mom Boula was Miss Athens 1957, dad relocated family to Covina, CA; Neil and Ratt's Stephen Pearcy called themselves "The Bordello Brothers."

NITRO

BIRTHPLACE: Los Angeles, CA
BANDMEMBERS: Jim Gillette (vocals), Michael Angelo (guitar), T.J. Racer (bass), Bobby Rock (drums)
ESSENTIAL HAIR CUTS: "Freight Train," "O.F.R."
FASCINATING FACTS: The most over-the-top Metal band ever, 1989's *O.F.R. (Out Fucking Rageous)* featured "the fastest guitars, highest screams, and loudest drums ever recorded"; for the album, Angelo designed the Quad Guitar X-400, built by Wayne Charvel, with four necks in an X formation, each neck with seven strings (a high A string, for an extra high octave); their bio read, "during Nitro concerts, Gillette shatters glass (imported crystal wine goblets) with a powerful, perfectly pitched scream. He has a six-octave range, sings with 10 different voices on *O.F.R.,* holds a 32-second scream, and sings a soprano high D which is devastating on equipment"; Angelo and Gillette known for Metal instructional videos—Angelo sold 100,000+ of his "Star Licks" video, the "Jim Gillette's Metal Power" series sold similar figures; album featured monstrous drummer Bobby Rock (Vinnie Vincent Invasion, Nelson); Gillette went on to marry Lita Ford.

POISON

BIRTHPLACE: Mechanicsburg, PA/ Los Angeles, CA
BANDMEMBERS: Bret Michaels (vocals), C.C. DeVille (guitar), Bobby Dahl (bass), Rikki Rockett (drums)
ESSENTIAL HAIR CUTS: "Talk Dirty To Me," "Nothin' But A Good Time," "Look What The Cat Dragged In," "Unskinny Bop," "Every Rose Has Its Thorn"
FASCINATING FACTS: The definitive Hair band; started back in PA in '83 as Paris; Bret, a famous diabetic, got the idea for using the colors black and lime green because he grew up six miles from Three Mile Island, and those are the nuclear colors; original guitarist Matt Smith replaced by Bay Ridge, Brooklyn-bred, NYU-dropout DeVille; C.C.'s parents ran a script service, and appeared in the "Talk Dirty To Me" video; Rockett, son of a trumpet player and a Rockette, supported himself as a hairdresser; Dahl, a licensed cosmetologist, the business man of the band; relentless self-promo got band signed to Enigma Records in 1986; work with Rick Rubin led to their Kiss cover ("Rock & Roll All Nite") on the *Less Than Zero* soundtrack; ballad "Something To Believe in" (at the time, MTV's longest-reigning #1 video) inspired by the death of Bret's friend/bodyguard James "Kimo the Flyin' Hawaiian" Maano; the original title to their second album *Open Up...And Say Ahh!* was rejected by the label—"Swallow This."

"WE GET TO HANG OUT WITH HOT CHICKS. IT'S FUCKIN' AWESOME!"

—Steve "Sex" Summers, Pretty Boy Floyd (1989)

PRETTY BOY FLOYD

BIRTHPLACE: Los Angeles, CA

BANDMEMBERS: Steve "Sex" Summers (vocals), Kristy Majors (guitar), Vinnie Chas (bass), Kari "The Mouth" Kane (drums)

ESSENTIAL HAIR CUTS: "Rock & Roll (Is Gonna Set The Night On Fire)," "Leather Boyz With Electric Toys," "Rock and Roll Outlaws"

FASCINATING FACTS: Self-professed purveyors of "Dirty Glam" the hottest band on the Sunset Strip circa 1988–89; their highly publicized debut, *Leather Boyz With Electric Toys* (MCA) sold respectable numbers (peaked #133 on the *Billboard* charts), but never achieved the smash success expected; amongst the few active bands still promoting a sleazy old-school vibe.

143

RATT

BIRTHPLACE: San Diego, CA/ Los Angeles, CA
BANDMEMBERS: Stephen Pearcy (vocals), Robbin Crosby (guitar), Warren DiMartini (guitar), Juan Croucier (bass), Bobby Blotzer (drums)
ESSENTIAL HAIR CUTS: "Round and Round," "Lay It Down," "You're In Love," "Way Cool Jr."
FASCINATING FACTS: Originally called Mickey Ratt, notorious in L.A. for their debauchery days at Ratt Mansion West; Tawny Kitaen, their childhood friend from San Diego, appeared on cover of *Out Of The Cellar,* their breakthrough LP with "Round and Round"; band managed by Milton Berle's nephew Marshall, the "Round and Round" video had Uncle Miltie in drag; Ratt later known for their concert contract rider, which required backstage posters of naked chicks, case of champagne, and a dozen condoms; Pearcy posed in *Playgirl;* Crosby died of AIDS in 2002.

"THERE ARE MUSICIANS WHO ARE YOUNG, GOOD-LOOKING, AND TALENTED, TOO. RATT IS LIVING PROOF."
—Robbin Crosby, Ratt (1986)

"PEOPLE MAKE FUN OF OUR NAME, BUT IS IT ANY WORSE THAN THE BEATLES? WE'RE NAMED AFTER A RODENT, AND THEY WERE NAMED AFTER A BUG."
—Stephen Pearcy, Ratt (1987)

144

LIGHTS OUT
SHE WON'T SHOUT
YOU'VE WON THE BOUT

—Roughhouse, "Midnight Madness"

"THE NAME
ROUGHHOUSE
COMES FROM HOW
WE ARE—LOUD, ROWDY
AND OBNOXIOUS."

—Mike Natalini, Roughhouse (1989)

BIRTHPLACE: Philadelphia, PA

BANDMEMBERS: Luis Rivera (vocals), Gregg Malack (guitar), Rex Eisen (guitar), Dave Weakley (bass), Mike Natalini (drums)

ESSENTIAL HAIR CUTS: "Teeze Me Pleeze Me," "Tonite"

FASCINATING FACTS: Originally called Teeze, a Crüe-style band with a huge suburban Philly following and well-received indie LP; name change came for legal reasons right after signing a "seven album deal" with Columbia, settling on this odd moniker; band-management conflicts led to a comedy of errors, including not shooting a video (for "Tonite") until two months after the album's release, which resulted in a flop record and a 1991 breakup.

145

ROXX GANG

"SOME PEOPLE WHO TAKE US STRICTLY ON OUR PHOTOS THINK WE'RE POSERS. THOSE PEOPLE NEED TO COME SEE US LIVE. YOU CANNOT SAY THAT WE DON'T ROCK HARD."

—Kevin Steele, Roxx Gang (1990)

BIRTHPLACE: Tampa, FL
BANDMEMBERS: Kevin Steele (vocals), Wade Hays (guitar), Jeff Taylor (guitar), Roby "Strychnine" Strine (bass), David James Blackshire (drums)
ESSENTIAL HAIR CUT: "Scratch My Back," "No Easy Way Out"
FASCINATING FACTS: First Metal act signed by Virgin Records, their Beau Hill-produced debut album sold over 250,000 copies; band forced their way out of Virgin deal, but never capitalized on that situation, and split up in 1991; terrific fashion sense.

SKID ROW

BIRTHPLACE: Toms River, NJ

BANDMEMBERS: Sebastian Bach (vocals), Dave "Snake" Sabo (guitar), Scotti Hill (guitar), Rachel Bolan (bass), Rob Affuso (drums)

ESSENTIAL HAIR CUTS: "Youth Gone Wild," "18 And Life," "I Remember You," "Slave To The Grind," "Piece Of Me"

FASCINATING FACTS: Sabo and Bolan met at work at Garden State Music in Toms River, NJ; Bolan played in infamous Jersey punk band Genocide, whose singer Bobby Ebz influenced GG Allin; Sabo knew Bon Jovi from the local scene, Jon invited the new band (with original singer David Fallon) to open for him in Bethlehem, PA, but that did not go over well; success came with the 1988 addition of Bach (Bierk), thanks to Rock photographer Mark Weiss; Bach, born April 3, 1968 in Freeport, Bahamas to hippie parents, grew up in Peterborough, Ontario but left home at age 15 for Toronto (where his underage drinking buddy was Ronnie Sweetheart of The Throbs); Bach's antics made waves, chiefly an onstage bottle-throwing incident in Springfield, MA (December 27, 1989, opening for Aerosmith), and the fallout over his MTV appearance wearing a t-shirt that read: "AIDS Kills Fags Dead."

SLAUGHTER

BIRTHPLACE: Los Angeles, CA

BANDMEMBERS: Mark Slaughter (vocals), Tim Kelly (guitar), Dana Strum (bass), Blas Elias (drums)

ESSENTIAL HAIR CUTS: "Up All Night," "Fly To The Angels"

FASCINATING FACTS: When Chrysalis Records dropped the Vinnie Vincent Invasion, they opted to retain singer Slaughter and bassist Strum to form their own band; Dana noted for his production work with Ozzy, and for finding him guitarists Randy Rhoades and Jake E. Lee; Mark was born on the fourth of July, and played guitar in the Oliver Stone film *Born On The Fourth Of July;* band wrote and recorded the theme song to *Bill and Ted's Bogus Journey;* they cited "L.A. girls, European metal and Domino's Pizza" as their main influences; Kelly was charged with narcotics trafficking in 1993, and died in a 1998 car accident.

"I WAKE UP ANY TIME BETWEEN 11 IN THE MORNING AND 4 IN THE AFTERNOON. SOMETIME WE HAVE TO GO OUT TO RADIO STATIONS, SOMETIME WE HAVE TO GO DOWN TO THE WHIRLPOOL IN THE HOTEL. THAT'S OUR JOB."

—Mark Slaughter, Slaughter (1990)

148

Slaughter with fans

STEELHEART

BIRTHPLACE: Norwalk, CT
BANDMEMBERS: Michael "The Kid" Matijevic (vocals), Chris Risola (guitar), Frank DiCostanzo (guitar), James Ward (bass), John Fowler (drums)
ESSENTIAL HAIR CUTS: "I'll Never Let You Go," "Rock 'N Roll (I Just Wanna)"
FASCINATING FACTS: Came from fusion of two CT cover bands, Red Alert and Rage Of Angels; came up with the name Steelheart in L.A., over beers and tacos at Barney's Beanery; soon after the success of power ballad "I'll Never Let You Go," a stage accident at McNichols Arena in Denver caused Matijevic serious head injuries and a four-year recovery; Matijevic revered as the biggest rock star in Croatia; his soaring vocals used in the film *Rock Star* with Mark Wahlberg (singer for the fictional band Steel Dragon); Matijevic also recorded and acted under the name of Mikey Steel.

149

"WE WERE *VERY* WILD, NOT JUST A LITTLE. WE WERE INTO BOOZE, DRUGS NOT SO MUCH. YOU COULD SAY WE WERE ALCOHOLICS. THEN—BOOM!—WE WERE CHRISTIANS. WE WOKE UP."

—**Michael Sweet, Stryper (1986)**

"WE ALL OWE SO MUCH TO THE POWER OF GOD, AND WE SEE NO REASON THAT HIS VIRTUES SHOULDN'T BE EXTOLLED THROUGH THE GREATEST MUSIC THERE IS, HEAVY METAL."

—**Michael Sweet, Stryper (1987)**

BIRTHPLACE: Buena Park, CA
BANDMEMBERS: Michael Sweet (vocals, guitar), Oz Fox (guitar), Tim Gaines (bass), Robert Sweet (drums)
ESSENTIAL HAIR CUTS: "To Hell With The Devil," "Honestly"
FASCINATING FACTS: Christian band famous for throwing Bibles into audience; originally called Roxx Regime, with C.C. DeVille on guitar; manager-mom Janice Sweet; Stryper stands for "Salvation Through Redemption Yielding Peace, Encouragement and Righteousness," the "Isaiah 53:5" under their logo is the biblical verse "by His stripes we are healed"; faced several press showdowns with "anti-Christian" bands like WASP and Slayer; unsuccessfully went Grunge circa 1990 with 'We Will Rock The Hell Out Of You" and cover of Earth, Wind & Fire's "Shining Star."

TNT

BIRTHPLACE: Trondheim, Norway
BANDMEMBERS: Tony Harnell (vocals), Ronni Le Tekro (guitar), Morty Black (bass), Morten "Diesel" Dahl (drums)
ESSENTIAL HAIR CUTS: "10,000 Lovers (In One)," "Everyone's A Star"
FASCINATING FACTS: Norwegian Bon Jovi; Harnell, a pro skater and avid surfer from San Diego, and son of an opera singer, he moved to New York for college, where, through producer Mike Varney, hooked up with this established Scandinavian Metal band (whose first album was sung entirely in Norwegian). 1987's epic *Tell No Tales* won the band a "Spellemannsprisen" (Norwegian Grammy) as the "Rock Group Of The Year."

"WHEN I LISTEN TO ROCK, I DON'T WANNA BE TOLD THAT THERE'S TERRORISTS AND SHIT LIKE THAT BECAUSE I ALREADY KNOW THAT."

—Tony Harnell, TNT (1986)

TRIXTER

BIRTHPLACE: Paramus, NJ
BANDMEMBERS: Peter Loran (vocals), Steve Brown (guitar), P.J. Farley (bass), Mark "Gus" Scott (drums)
ESSENTIAL HAIR CUTS: "Give It To Me Good," "Bad Girl"
FASCINATING FACTS: Teeny-bop-style one-hit wonders; their Paul Rachman-produced video for "Give It To Me Good," a Top 40 single that went #1 on *Dial MTV*, played suburban house parties for six years in New Jersey before they got signed at age 18; opened for Stryper, Dokken, Poison, and Warrant.

"WITH TRIXTER, THE BOYS JUST WANNA HAVE FUN!"
—**Peter Loran, Trixter (1990)**

153

"OUR CROWD USED TO BE 70–80% GIRLS, BUT NOW WE'RE GETTING MORE GUYS TO COME OUT—THEY'RE GOING BECAUSE OF ALL THE GIRLS!"

—Michael Lean, Tuff (1989)

TUFF

BIRTHPLACE: Phoenix, AZ/ Los Angeles, CA
BANDMEMBERS: Stevie Rachelle (vocals), Jorge DeSaint (guitar), Todd Chase (bass), Michael Lean (drums)
ESSENTIAL HAIR CUTS: "The All New Generation," "I Hate Kissing You Goodbye"
FASCINATING FACTS: "The last of the Hair bands," their 1991 debut album *What Comes Around… Goes Around* (Titanium/ Atlantic) had the power ballad "I Hate Kissing You Goodbye," an MTV hit around the same time as Nirvana's "Smells Like Teen Spirit"; Bret Michaels wrote ballad "Wake Me Up" for the album; Tuff formed in Phoenix in 1985, with original singer Jim Gillette, who went on to Nitro; by 1987, band moved to L.A., where they teamed up with Oshkosh, WI native Rachelle; Stevie still flies the Hair flag with his popular website www.metalsludge.com.

"DAVY VAIN *IS* ROCK AND ROLL. SEX AND ROCK & ROLL. HE'S INCAPABLE OF ANYTHING ELSE EXCEPT WRITING SONGS OR FUCKING CHICKS OR PERFORMING ONSTAGE. HE'S THE DEFINITION OF A ROCK SINGER, HE REALLY IS. THE POOR GUY WILL HAVE A FUCKING HARD-ON TILL HIS DYING DAY."

—Ashley Mitchell, Vain (1989)

VAIN

BIRTHPLACE: San Francisco, CA

BANDMEMBERS: Davy Vain (vocals), Danny West (guitar), James Scott (guitar), Ashley Mitchell (bass), Tommy Rickard (drums)

ESSENTIAL HAIR CUT: "Beat The Bullet"

FASCINATING FACTS: Davy produced two albums for noted Bay Area thrash band Death Angel; first and only Hair band on Island Records; Davy on the cover of *Kerrang!* before ever signing a record deal; band dropped before their second album could ever come out; for a short time at their end, included GN'R's Steven Adler.

155

VINNIE VINCENT

"WHEN I WAS A MEMBER OF THAT UN-NAMED BAND [KISS] A FEW YEARS AGO, I KNEW SOONER OR LATER I WAS GONNA HAVE TO BREAK AWAY ON MY OWN AND TRY THINGS THEY WOULDN'T ALLOW..."

—Vinnie Vincent, Vinnie Vincent Invasion (1987)

BIRTHPLACE: Los Angeles, CA
BANDMEMBERS: Mark Slaughter (vocals), Vinnie Vincent (guitar), Dana Strum (bass), Bobby Rock (drums)
ESSENTIAL HAIR CUTS: "Boyz Are Gonna Rock," "Love Kills"
FASCINATING FACTS: Vinnie Vincent (Cusano), from Bridgeport, CT, became known as songwriter for TV series "Happy Days"; later replaced Ace Frehley as Kiss guitarist, played both with makeup on and off, and co-wrote their comeback hits "Lick It Up" and "All Hell's Breaking Loose"; Vinnie then signed a much-hyped eight-album, $4M solo deal; new band a colossal failure as Vinnie's Kiss songs were catchy "dance metal" while VVI was two albums of shrill guitar hero worship; Vinnie had a bad reputation in the business, VVI's last straw came when the band's gear was seized in a legal dispute, allegedly for over-extending his credit from the label; Mark Slaughter and Dana Strum went on to form Slaughter.

156

VIXEN

BIRTHPLACE: St. Paul, MN/Los Angeles, CA
BANDMEMBERS: Janet Gardner (vocals), Jan Lynn Kuehnemund (guitar), Share Pedersen (bass), Roxy Petrucci (drums)
ESSENTIAL HAIR CUTS: "Edge Of A Broken Heart," "Cryin'"
FASCINATING FACTS: Vixen's self-titled debut album, with the hit single "Edge Of A Broken Heart" (written by Richard Marx and Fee Waybill), the first time an all-female band went gold; original bassist Pia Maiocco married Steve Vai; band started by Jan Kuehnemund (pronounced keen-a-min) in St. Paul, MN, later joined by fellow L.A. club scene vet Petrucci, whose sister Maxine Petrucci played in Madam X ("High In High School"); Pederson later played in short-lived quasi-supergroup Contraband.

"IF YOU DON'T GET A HARD-ON LISTENING TO US, YOU'D BETTER GO SEE A DOCTOR."
—Roxy Petrucci, Vixen (1991)

157

WARRANT

BIRTHPLACE: Van Nuys, CA
BANDMEMBERS: Jani Lane (vocals), Joey Allen (guitar), Erik Turner (guitar), Jerry Dixon (bass), Steven Sweet (drums)
ESSENTIAL HAIR CUTS: "Down Boys," "Cherry Pie," "Heaven," "Sometime She Cries"
FASCINATING FACTS: Warrant "named after" Ratt's Warren DiMartini; Lane started in suburban Cleveland as drummer/solo act Mitch Dynamite; Warrant notorious on Sunset Strip for their lurid flyers, particularly scratch-and-sniff flyers; first show Sept. 27, 1986; now-famous artist Mark Ryden did cover for their debut, *Dirty Rotten Filthy Stinking Rich;* Columbia rejected *Vertical Smile* as title for their second album, settling on *Cherry Pie.*

"YOU ALWAYS HATE YOUR OWN HAIR, BUT I WOULDN'T WANNA BE BALD DOING THIS!"

—Steven Sweet, Warrant (1989)

160

"WE'RE A ROCK AND ROLL BAND OF THE '80s—HERE TODAY, HERE TO STAY, HERE TOMORROW!"

—Mike Tramp, White Lion (1988)

WHITE LION

BIRTHPLACE: Brooklyn, New York

BANDMEMBERS: Mike Tramp (vocals), Vito Bratta (guitar), James Lomenzo (bass), Greg D'Angelo (drums)

ESSENTIAL HAIR CUTS: "Wait," "When The Children Cry"

FASCINATING FACTS: Referred to themselves as kings of "Rock and Roar"; Tramp (Trampeneu) from Denmark, played at L'Amour in Brooklyn with his band Mabel (who, on the plane ride to JFK Airport, changed their name to White Lion), where they opened for Bratta's band Dreamer; White Lion later rehearsed at L'Amour; debut album *Fight To Survive*, an underground classic in Europe, was dropped by Elektra before its domestic release, later came out on indie Grand Slamm; Tramp's flashy stagewear created by girlfriend/costume designer Fleur Thiemeyer; Lomenzo replaced both one-time Sabbath bassist Dave "The Animal" Spitz (brother of Anthrax's Danny Spitz) and Bruno Ravel, later of Danger Danger; D'Angelo played in an early lineup of Anthrax, and in the Hardcore Punk band Ism.

Mike Tramp of White Lion

WHITESNAKE

BIRTHPLACE: London, England/ Los Angeles, CA

BANDMEMBERS: David Coverdale (vocals), Adrian Vandenburg (guitar), Vivian Campbell (guitar), Rudy Sarzo (bass); Tommy Aldrich (drums)

ESSENTIAL HAIR CUTS: "Here I Go Again," "Still Of The Night"

FASCINATING FACTS: Coverdale came to prominence as the Deep Purple singer who replaced Ian Gillan, vocalist on their hit "Burn"; Whitesnake's mega album, 1987's *Whitesnake*, employed a host of studio musicians, notably guitarist John Sykes (Thin Lizzy, Blue Murder); David credited his success to an operation for a deviated septum, and to voice-strengthening lessons with Jewish cantor Nathan Lam; Coverdale married actress Tawny Kitaen (star of the "Still Of The Night" video), a much-hyped, short-lived union; lineup for follow-up *Slip Of The Tongue* saw guitar god Steve Vai replacing Campbell, before egos imploded.

161

David Coverdale of Whitesnake with Tawny Kitaen

WILD BOYZ

BIRTHPLACE: Los Angeles, CA
BANDMEMBERS: Willie D. (vocals), Valentino (guitar), Matt Steavanz (guitar) Joey Wylde (bass), K. Lee Lauren (drums)
ESSENTIAL HAIR CUTS: "Pleazure 'N' Pain," "High Tonight"
FASCINATING FACT: Sunset Strip act first called Dorian Gray.

SUGAR'Z GOT THAT CANDY-COATED LUVIN' YEAH HOLD ON TIGHT SHE'Z A HURRICANE CUMIN'!

—Wild Boyz, "Take Me"

"KIP'S A GREAT LOOKING GUY, AND HE'S VERY QUICKLY BECOMING A SEX SYMBOL TO THE LITTLE GIRLS. WE WENT TO THE MALL THE OTHER DAY AND HAD TO BE USHERED OUT BY SECURITY GUYS, OR WE WERE NEVER GONNA GET OUT OF THERE!"

—Paul Taylor, Winger (1989)

**SHE'S ONLY SEVENTEEN
DADDY SAYS SHE'S TOO YOUNG
BUT SHE'S OLD ENOUGH FOR ME**

—Winger, "Seventeen"

"I CAN'T HELP THE WAY I LOOK! I MEAN, I DIDN'T HAVE BRACES AND I DON'T HAVE A NOSE JOB... IT'S GOOD, BUT IT CAN ALSO BE A PROBLEM."

—Kip Winger, Winger (1989)

WINGER

BIRTHPLACE: New York, NY

BANDMEMBERS: Kip Winger (vocals, bass), Reb Beach (guitar), Rod Morgenstein (drums), Paul Taylor (keyboards)

ESSENTIAL HAIR CUTS: "Madalaine," "Seventeen," "Easy Come Easy Go," "Miles Away"

FASCINATING FACTS: Kip Winger (Charles Von Winger) from Colorado, played in family band The Wingerz; Kip studied ballet and orchestra in New York City, where he worked on the *Hearts Of Fire* soundtrack; came to prominence as bass player for Alice Cooper (the mid-'80s lineup with Rambo-looking Kane Roberts on guitar); Winger, the band, featured esteemed Dixie Dregs drummer Rod Morgenstein; Kip threatened legal action against MTV for his portrayal in "Beavis & Butthead."

ADAM BOMB	"I WANT MY HEAVY METAL"	**EVERY MOTHER'S NIGHTMARE**	"WALLS COME DOWN"
ASPHALT BALLET	"HELL'S KITCHEN"	**EUROPE**	"ROCK THE NIGHT"
BABYLON AD	"BANG GO THE BELLS"	**EZO**	"FLASHBACK HEART ATTACK"
BADLANDS	"HIGH WIRE"	**FEMME FATALE**	"WAITING FOR THE BIG ONE"
BANGALORE CHOIR	"JUST ONE NIGHT"	**FIREHOUSE**	"DON'T TREAT ME BAD"
BANG TANGO	"SOMEONE LIKE YOU"	**HELIX**	"HEAVY METAL LOVE"
BATON ROUGE	"WALKS LIKE A WOMAN"	**HERICANE ALICE**	"WILD YOUNG AND CRAZY"
BEAU NASTY	"PARADISE IN THE SAND"	**HURRICANE**	"I'M ONTO YOU"
CANDY	"AMERICAN KIX"	**JACKYL**	"I STAND ALONE"
CATS N BOOTS	"NINE LIVES (SAVE ME)"	**JETBOY**	"FEEL THE SHAKE"
CHILD'S PLAY	"DAY AFTER NIGHT"	**JOHNNY CRASH**	"THRILL OF THE KILL"
COLD SWEAT	"FOUR ON THE FLOOR"	**JUNKYARD**	"HOLLYWOOD"
CRY WOLF	"PRETENDER"	**KIK TRACEE**	"VELVET CRUSH"
DANGEROUS TOYS	"TEAS'N PLEAS'N"	**KISS**	"LICK IT UP"
DIAMOND REXX	"LADIES NIGHT"	**LAW AND ORDER**	"WE DON'T SEE GOD"
DIRTY BLONDE	"GIRLS NIGHT OUT"	**LILLIAN AXE**	"SHE LIKES IT ON TOP"
DIRTY LOOKS	"COOL FROM THE WIRE"	**LONDON**	"DROP THE BOMB"
DIRTY RHYTHM	"HOT N' COLD"	**LOVE/HATE**	"ROCK QUEEN"
D'MOLLS	"D'STROLL"	**LYNCH MOB**	"WICKED SENSATION"
ELECTRIC ANGELS	"RATTLESNAKE KISSES"	**MCQUEEN STREET**	"IN HEAVEN"
ELECTRIC BOYS	"ALL LIPS AND HIPS"	**PRINCESS PANG**	"TROUBLE IN PARADISE"
		ROCK CITY ANGELS	"TEENAGE LIPSTICK BOYS"
		ROXY BLUE	"TOO HOT TO HANDLE"

MORE ESSENTIAL HAIR CUTS

SAIGON KICK	"COME TAKE ME NOW"
SALTY DOG	"RING MY BELL"
SARAYA	"LOVE HAS TAKEN ITS TOLL"
THE SCREAM	"OUTLAW"
SEA HAGS	"BACK TO THE GRIND"
SHARK ISLAND	"BAD FOR EACH OTHER"
SHOTGUN MESSIAH	"SQUEEZIN' TEAZIN'"
SILENT RAGE	"REBEL WITH A CAUSE"
SKIN AND BONES	"NAIL IT DOWN"
SLEEZE BEEZ	"GIRLS GIRLS NASTY NASTY"
SMASHED GLADYS	"DIVE IN THE DARK"
SOUTHGANG	"TAINTED ANGEL"
SPREAD EAGLE	"SWITCHBLADE SERENADE"
SVEN GALI	"UNDER THE INFLUENCE"
SWEET F.A.	"PRINCE OF THE CITY"
SWEET PAIN	"I GET MY KICKS"
TANGIER	"RIP CORD"
TATTOOED LOVE BOYS	"READ MY LIPS"
TESLA	"MODERN DAY COWBOY"
THE THROBS	"COME DOWN SISTER"
TIGERTAILZ	"STAR ATTRACTION"
TORA TORA	"WALKIN' SHOES"
TYKETTO	"FOREVER YOUNG"
WILDSIDE	"KISS THIS LOVE GOODBYE"
XYZ	"INSIDE OUT"
Y&T	"SUMMERTIME GIRLS"
ZEBRA	"TELL ME WHAT YOU WANT"

Ronnie Sweetheart of The Throbs

SOURCES

.45 Dangerous Minds: The Most Intense Interviews From Seconds Magazine, 2005.

100 Metal Pix: Giant Superspecial, April 1990.

Best of Rock Scene #6, January 1989.

Blast!, July 1989.

Circus, May 31, 1984; November 30, 1985; March 31, 1986; April 30, 1986; November 17, 1986; November 30, 1986; December 31, 1986; June 30, 1987; December 31, 1987; January 31, 1988; April 30, 1988; May 31, 1988; July 31, 1988; October 31, 1988; November 30, 1988; December 31, 1988; February 28, 1989; March 31, 1989; May 31, 1989; July 31, 1989; August 31, 1989; September 30, 1989; November 30, 1989; December 31, 1989; January 31, 1990; April 30, 1990; May 31, 1990; August 31, 1990; September 30, 1990; November 30, 1990; December 31, 1990; May 31, 1991.

Concert Shots, #6, May 1986.

Concrete Foundations, Vol 1, #23, 1988; Volume 2, #5, 1989.

Creem Metal Close-Up, March 1986; March 1987; April 1987; August 1987; June 1988; July 1988.

Frank 151, #20.

Hard Rock's Metal Studs, Movie Screen Yearbook #35.

Hit Parader, January 1987; February 1987; November 1987; November 1990.

Metal Edge, November 1987; December 1987.

Metallion, Vol 2, #11, 1986.

Metallix, #2, 1987; #4, 1988, #5, 1988.

Mötley Crüe Magazine, Superstar Facts & Pix #11, 1987.

Musician, May 1995.

Paper Magazine, September 1998.

Powerline, July 1989.

RIP, January, 1991.

Rock Of The 80s II, #6, 1988.

Rock Of The 80s III, July, 1989.

Rock Of The 90s, Spotlight #12, 1989; March 1990.

Rock Scene Collector's Edition, Vol 5 #1, January 1990.

Rocking Into The 90s, Vol 1, 1989.

The Scene, #1, 1988; #2, 1989; #3, 1990.

Seconds, #22, 1992; #23, 1993; #26, 1994; #28, 1994; #45, 1997.

Spin, December, 1991.

Special thanks for research assistance: www.sleazeroxx.com

168

Above: Poison and photographer Frank White backstage, Right: Mick Sweda of King Kobra

169

Above: Poison, Right: Tommy Lee of Mötley Crüe

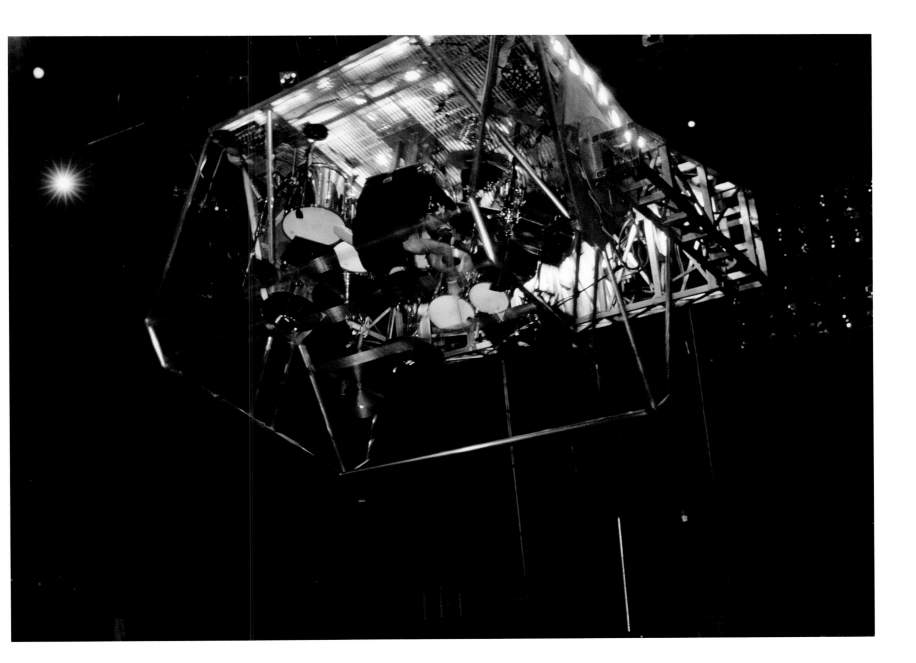

CREDITS

Fred Berger: page 35 (L), 110

William Hames: page 2, 9, 21, 23, 24, 27, 28, 29, 30, 31, 43, 48, 50, 52, 56, 59, 64, 67, 68, 70, 73, 75, 79, 80, 82, 87, 99, 114, 117, 118, 119, 123, 128, 136, 139, 142, 143, 146, 149, 152, 154, 156, 170, 171

Bob Leafe: page 168

Mark Leialoha: page 155

Mark Leivdahl: cover, page 16, 58, 140, 141

Eddie Malluk: page 5, 17 (R), 20, 22, 25, 30, 33, 34, 36, 44, 49 (L), 54, 57, 60, 61, 66, 69, 74, 76, 83, 91, 94, 94, 96, 98, 105, 116, 120, 121, 124 (R), 125, 127, 129, 133, 137, 138, 144, 147, 151, 153, 159, 161, 163, 167, 174, 176

Christine Natanael: page 106

Debra Trebitz: page 28

Frank White: page 6, 10, 12, 13, 14, 15, 17 (L), 35, 37, 40 (L, C, R), 41 (L, C, R,), 42, 45, 46, 47, 49 (R, L), 51, 63, 71, 72, 78, 88, 89, 90, 93, 113, 122, 124 (L), 130, 134, 135, 157, 158, 160, 165, 169, 173

Illustration Credits
Wendy Vaught: page 100 (Tom Keifer/Cinderella)
Hydie Debald: page 102 (Michael Sweet/Stryper)
Sabrina Guiles: page 103 (Stephen Pearcy/Ratt)
Carolyn Bennett: page 100 (Bret Michaels/Poison)
Cory Hillman: page 100 (Jon Bon Jovi)
Craig Davidson: page 103 (Gun's N' Roses)

Rock Comics
Greg Fox: page 108 (Poison)
Larry Nadolsky: page (Mötley Crüe)

Backstage Passes: collection of Frank White

ABOUT THE AUTHOR

Steven Blush has written two books on the subject of Rock: *American Hardcore: A Tribal History* (Feral House, 2001), a history of the early-'80s Hardcore Punk scene, and *.45 Dangerous Minds* (Creation Books, 2005), a collection of interviews with Pop Culture's most notorious characters.

Blush's writings have appeared in over 25 publications, including *Spin, Details, Interview, Village Voice,* and *The Times Of London.* For 15 years, he published the cult magazine *Seconds*, and currently serves as contributing editor at *Paper.*

He lives in Manhattan, where he is a DJ and promoter of NYC's longest-running Rock party "Röck Cändy". Blush is writer/producer of the Sony Picture Classics-distributed documentary film *American Hardcore,* inspired by the Feral House book of the same name.

175

Left: Keel, Following page: Mike Tramp of White Lion